DISCOVERING STOICISM

A BEGINNER'S JOURNEY TO INNER PEACE

MASSIMO HOLIDAY

DESERT WORDS LLC

INTRODUCTION

Whenever two or more people are discussing issues of personal well-being, happiness, contentment, character, success, grit, confidence, wisdom, and resiliency, the conversation will inadvertently lead to stoicism, an old philosophy that can significantly change how you live your life.

When you adopt stoicism and make its philosophy, principles, and practice an integral part of your daily life, in addition to improving your overall well-being and happiness, you will also develop a desirable character, become wiser, confident, and more successful in every area of your life including relationship and business.

If this assertion seems 'too promising,' consider this. Most successful people such as Warren Buffet, Bill Gates, Jeff Bezos, Elon Musk, Tim Ferriss, Theodore Roosevelt, Bill Clinton, Thomas Jefferson, Ralph Waldo Emerson, Arnold Schwarzenegger, J.K Rowling, and many, many other wildly successful and famous individuals practice elements of stoicism.

The assertion here is not that becoming stoic or adopting its practices will automatically lead to success, no. The argument is that by internalizing stoic principles and applying stoic philosophies to your life, your character will change for the better, and your life will take on new meaning.

What exactly is stoicism, though? What are its teachings, core principles, and philosophies? Given the ancient nature of stoicism, do its practices fit into our modern-day environment, and how best can you implement these practices to enhance your overall well-being, life, and the lives of those you hold dear?

This book is your guide to stoicism and to various means of practicing it in your life. In the following pages, you will discover why stoicism remains a significant value even in modern, technology-dominated, and consume-oriented times like ours.

Let's get started!

1

WHAT IS STOICISM?

Stoicism is simply a wisdom philosophy that teaches you how to live a good life. Every person wishes to live a happy life, and Stoicism seeks to increase your happiness. Stoicism is an approachable philosophy. In fact, since its inception, Stoicism has been the only philosophy that has addressed all humans. All genders, races, and social classes were considered equal in the Stoic philosophy. This explains why Stoicism has lasted over 2300 years. People of all races, socioeconomic backgrounds, and cultures find it acceptable. It has evolved in tandem with humanity.

Stoicism has the most practical and applicable rules for all artists, writers, and business owners. Their focus is always drawn to two issues:

- How to live a happy, fulfilling, and wonderful life
- How to turn yourself into a better person

The main goal is to achieve inner peace by acknowledging that we only have a limited time on Earth, being aware of our impulses, exercising self-control, and overcoming adversity. These are meditative practices that will help us live in harmony with nature rather than in opposition to it. We must understand the challenges we face and never run away from them. They need to be turned into fuel for our fires.

According to Stoic philosophy, nothing can be considered good or bad. Everything is down to our perception and judgment. Virtue is the only good thing in the world and the highest ideal for everyone to strive. Stoics believe that while evil does not exist in nature, it is caused by human behavior. People who cause harm lack virtue and refuse to follow nature's laws.

The highest ideal for Stoics is to cultivate a noble personality. This is unrelated to money or social standing. It is only possible if you live in harmony with nature and strive for virtue in everything you do.

Stoicism's unique charm and value are its accessibility and applicability, which make it so important and easy to practice even today. The main goal of Stoicism was to be free of suffering and to be able to endure life's highs and lows.

The Origins of Stoicism

The history of Stoicism goes back to 301 BC, and starts with a man called Zeno about 2,300 years ago in the Greek capital of Athens. Zeno of Cyprus was a merchant who survived a shipwreck but lost everything he gained throughout his life. At this point most of us would give up and blame the circumstances, but not Zeno. He turned these events into a new start in his life. By searching and studying, he developed a unique approach to life, which became the foundation of Stoicism and its teachings. Zeno studied philosophy under the Cynics for several years before becoming a student at Plato's Academy. After that, he decided to start his own school in Athens's central market. Zeno used to stand on the porch and talk to any person who happened to be passing by. He gave lectures regarding principles of personal ethics. Soon he began educating others. It was here where Stoicism got its name. Unlike other philosophers, Zeno was much more open and taught in public.

Over time, he drew a crowd of men who would regularly stand with him and talk about philosophy. For the next 500 years, Stoicism was transformed from a philosophy adopted by a bunch of idle men into the foremost philosophy in ancient Greece and Rome. During the Renaissance, its popularity soared again as more people searched for deeper answers on how to live life.

The Three Stoic Disciplines

Desire

The first of the three Stoic disciplines is that of desire. At the time Zeno was working out the shape of his philosophy, several traditions addressed the issue of human desire and the consequences it produced. Some of these traditions encouraged a reckless abandon to primal urges, stating that life is to be enjoyed to the fullest regardless of the consequences. In contrast, other traditions sought to virtually purge the human spirit of any primal desires, choosing instead to live a life of austerity and asceticism, thus avoiding all consequences of desire completely. Zeno recognized that while such extreme measures might help a person to avoid a certain level of suffering, they did not offer any meaningful peace or contentment. Allowing oneself to indulge in vice without guilt might remove shame and regret, but it would not provide lasting joy in life. Alternatively, depriving oneself of pleasure, although an effective way of preventing guilt and shame, was no way to find happiness. Therefore, a solution somewhere between the two extremes needed to be found. The Discipline of Desire was the Stoic answer to this dilemma.

Action

The second of the three Stoic disciplines is the Discipline of Action. Zeno perceived that many other traditions failed to have any meaningful impact on the human condition because they treated desire as the single root cause of suffering. While untamed desire can be seen as a significant cause of much, if not most human suffering, it is not the only cause. Zeno understood that action was just as responsible for suffering as desire. This can be demonstrated by the fact that even though an individual may only pursue rational desires, they may still use irrational means to achieve them. An easy way to portray this is if a person wants to raise money for a charity. No one would ever argue that raising money for a charity is anything but a noble and worthwhile thing to do. This would make it a rational desire. However, if a person achieved their goal by robbing banks and committing such acts as embezzlement, extortion, and the like, then a great deal of suffering would necessarily ensue. Thus, the axiom "the ends justify the means" was not one that Zeno would have found particularly accurate. Instead, just as an individual needs to hone and cultivate their desires, so too, they must also hone and cultivate the nature of their actions.

Assent

A perfect example of this can be found in farming. The location of a farm will determine the crops that can be grown there. Knowing what plants will grow in a particular place is the logical aspect of this discipline. However, accepting that you can only grow certain crops is the Discipline of Assent. The wise farmer focuses on the plants that he knows will thrive in the conditions available to his farm. He spends his time and energy cultivating those plants to produce the best possible results. And this usually leads to a successful harvest every year. However, if a farmer were to reject the limitations created by the farm's location and plant whatever he wanted, then the results would be far less favorable. Instead of harvesting loads of healthy fruits and vegetables, the farmer would have little or nothing to show for his efforts. While other plants might make more money, if they won't grow in his area, then there is no point in planting them. Thus, the farmer must accept that certain crops are beyond his capability to grow and must therefore devote his efforts to what he knows are more reasonable and realistic goals.

Four Virtues of Stoicism

Wisdom

The first of the Stoic virtues is that of wisdom. This is yet another example of where the original meaning of a word could be more understood in translation. In modern-day usage, wisdom usually refers to a general sense of knowledge and understanding. Older or more experienced people are often characterized as wise because they know more about a specific thing or life in general.

In essence, the virtues are the total of a field plus a discipline. In this case, wisdom is the byproduct of logic and assent. Logic was the tool by which the Stoic could study life and learn the lessons it possessed, and assent was the discipline that enabled the individual to distinguish between what was controllable and what was not. By applying logic and assent to daily life, the Stoic could develop a strong sense of insight regarding the true nature of things. And this insight, or practical wisdom, would enable them to make more rational choices, take more effective actions, and live a more purpose-driven and meaningful life.

Justice

Justice is the second of the Stoic virtues. One way to get an idea of the original meaning intended for this virtue is to see it with its corresponding field and discipline. Ethics is the field of study connected to justice, and action is the discipline. Combined, ethics and the Discipline of Action form a sense of what is right and a duty to abide by that sense. Thus, while ethics contains the knowledge of proper behavior, and the Discipline of Action helps the individual to act accordingly, the end result is a life lived in justice. Again, the purpose of the virtue is to personify the ideal created by the other aspects of Stoicism. Therefore, rather than blindly following the concepts of ethics and action, a Stoic practitioner can follow them with a real sense of direction, envisioning the final destination that devoted practice will lead to.

· · ·

Temperance

Understanding this aspect of temperance is critical for understanding why it was chosen as a Stoic virtue in the first place. At the time of Zeno, there were several traditions that sought to resolve the debate over the issue of pleasure. Some believed all pleasures were good and should be aimed at all times. Others stated that pleasure was the root of suffering and evil and should thus be avoided at every opportunity. Zeno believed that the true solution could be between indulgence and abstinence. The result was the concept of temperance, ultimately defined by the axiom "all things in moderation."

Courage

The fourth of the Stoic virtues is that of courage. Much like the field of logic, which is the tool needed to study all other aspects of Stoicism, courage is the tool that the Stoic needs to achieve all other virtues. Courage is the tool needed to follow the Stoic path in any meaningful way. It can be all too easy to abandon the way of Stoicism and surrender to desire, greed, and even fear. Additionally, it is easy to follow the crowd and do what everyone else is doing, regardless of whether it is right or wrong. However, following the Stoic tradition takes a great deal of courage. The practitioner must be brave enough not only to face criticism and resistance from the outside but also to face the temptations, weaknesses, and demons found within. Therefore, one must have the necessary courage and fortitude to pursue Stoicism.

2

———

A QUICK TRIP THROUGH HISTORY

To understand stoicism, it's helpful to learn a bit of history and how it emerged. Stoicism originates from ancient Greeks in 300 BCE, but the philosophy we now know filtered through later Romans. Looking into the lives of the people who developed the philosophy can help us appreciate it in new ways. Stoics were real people, the same as us. If they could create and practice a philosophy of human flourishing, we can as well. Let's meet some of the people behind it!

Before Stoicism

Before Zeno of Citium developed the philosophy that became Stoicism, he studied quite a few philosophies. His first influence came from the Cynic teacher, Crates. One of the Cynics' core tenets will sound familiar: The purpose of life is to live in virtue. Cynics practiced virtue by rejecting more conventional desires. Zeno also studied Platonism under Xenocrates and Polemon. Like Plato's followers, Zeno held Socrates up as an exemplary human. The Stoics considered themselves direct philosophical descendants of Socrates. Zeno also studied the Megarians, who may have influenced his belief in the unity of virtue. From these rich influences and more, Zeno developed something new, a philosophy that thrived for 500 years and has never fully left us.

First Philosophers

The people whose influence on Stoicism lives on today include the following, listed chronologically from the earliest to the most recent.

Zeno (CIRCA 334–262 BCE)

What we know of Zeno of Citium, the founder of Stoicism, comes from a biography by ancient historian Diogenes Laertius. One story about his younger life says, "He consulted the oracle to know what he should do to attain the best life, and that the god's response was that he should take on the complexion of the dead." Zeno decided this meant he should study ancient writers, and it's through this that his love of philosophy blossomed.

According to Diogenes Laertius, Zeno was a merchant sailing with his goods when a storm left him shipwrecked. Unsure what to do in life, Zeno made his way to Athens, went to a bookseller, and read an account of Socrates' life. Impressed by what he learned, Zeno asked the bookseller where he could find people like Socrates. At that moment, a famous Cynic philosopher, Crates of Thebes, passed by. The bookseller pointed and said, "Follow him."

· · ·

We may not know exactly how it happened, but we know Zeno arrived in Athens around 312 BCE and that by 300 BCE he started the Stoic school. His own philosophy retained the threefold division of logic, physics, and ethics from his Platonist days, though his physics differed significantly from that of Plato. His ethics retained much from the Cynics, though the Stoics were less dramatic in their asceticism.

Zeno wrote many books, but today we only have titles. Early Stoic works were lost to philosophical purges where books were burned, to general neglect, and to the ravages of time. What we know of Zeno comes in glimpses from quotes and other fragments. We know that Zeno wrote The Republic, a book that described a perfect Stoic world. Zeno made bold claims for his time: He insisted that all people should be seen as equal citizens, which included equality among men and women. Zeno believed that all people had equal access to virtue, but few ever perfected it. Socrates, Diogenes, and the mythic Hercules were some of the few people he held up as sages, the truly virtuous. This might be why the early name, Zenonians, never stuck: Zeno never claimed to be perfect. Instead, the school was named for the place it was taught—the Stoa—where lessons were open to anyone.

Aristo of Chios (CIRCA 300–CIRCA 260 BCE)

Aristo was a contemporary of Zeno. His philosophy shows the wide divergence of Stoic thought from its origins. Aristo believed that only ethics mattered. His views did not prevail, as Zeno's ideas were solidified by the third head of the Stoic school, Chrysippus, and became Stoicism proper. Even though Aristo seemingly lost that ancient battle, I find that his choice to drop logic and physics to emphasize practical ethics fits with our modern spirit.

Cleanthes (CIRCA 330–CIRCA 230 BCE)

After he died, Zeno bequeathed his school to one of his students, Cleanthes. Cleanthes began life as a boxer but switched careers to become a philosopher after hearing Zeno's lectures. Cleanthes valued physical labor and supported himself both as a student and later as the second head of the school through hard toil. He worked nights as a water carrier for a gardener, irrigating the land by walking from the well to the garden and back again. Cleanthes kept the Stoa for over 30 years, expanding and solidifying a variety of Zeno's doctrines. Zeno told his pupils to "live consistently." Cleanthes added, "with nature." He supposedly wrote more than 50 works, but again, we only have fragments. One of the longest works that we still have is called "Hymn to Zeus," which gives us an idea of the Stoic relationship with their god, the universe. This prayer was just a part of his hymn:

"To wherever your decrees have assigned me.
   I follow readily, but if I choose not,
   Wretched though I am, I must follow still.
   Fate guides the willing, but drags the unwilling."

Chrysippus (CIRCA 279–CIRCA 206 BCE)

Chrysippus was Cleanthes's student and the third head of the Stoic school. We know that he was a brilliant philosopher and that he greatly expanded on Zeno's teachings, so much so that he is called the Second Founder of Stoicism. Diogenes Laertius said, "Without Chrysippus, there would be no Stoa."

Cicero (106–43 BCE)

In 155 BCE, the head of the Stoic school, accompanied by other philosophers, went to Rome. They made such a strong impression that in the mid-40s BCE a famous Roman statesman and orator, Cicero, wrote multiple books about Stoic ideas. He did not consider himself a Stoic, citing differences with their physics and other ideas, but he practiced Stoic ethics, and his works pass on information that otherwise would have been lost.

Seneca (4 BCE–65 CE)

Seneca was also a Roman statesman who famously advised Emperor Nero in the early years of Nero's reign. Seneca was a practicing Stoic and, as a prolific writer, wrote 124 letters on morality and a variety of essays that constitute one of the more important bodies of Stoic thought to which we still have access.

Musonius Rufus (CIRCA 30–100 CE)

Musonius Rufus was the teacher of a better-known Stoic, Epictetus. We have a small collection of his lectures, which illuminate Stoic thoughts on a range of subjects, such as what

Stoics should eat, how they should dress and furnish their homes, and their relationship to work and family. Epictetus states that his teacher did not want students to praise his words, but to be stunned into contemplative silence. As Musonius said, "The philosopher's school is a doctor's office. You must leave not pleased, but pained."

Epictetus (55–135 CE)

We know of Epictetus because a student, Arrian, transcribed his lectures in the Discourses and the Enchiridion. Epictetus started life as a slave, was given his freedom, and became a Stoic teacher. His influence on modern Stoicism is hard to overestimate: He likely developed the three Disciplines. A true Stoic, Epictetus always focused on changing the lives of his students. He didn't want them to mistake memorization of Stoic texts for the real work of building a better self. "If you are acting in harmony, show me that," he said, "and I will tell you that you are making progress; but if out of harmony, begone, and do not confine yourself to expounding your books, heck, go and write some books yourself. And what will you gain?"

Marcus Aurelius (121 CE–180 CE)

"Not to feel exasperated or defeated or despondent because your days aren't packed with wise and moral actions. But to get back up when you fail, to celebrate behaving like a human—however imperfectly—and fully embrace the pursuit you've embarked on." —Marcus Aurelius, Meditations 5:9

From 161 to 180 CE, Roman emperor Marcus Aurelius kept a personal philosophical journal. That journal, now often titled Meditations, is one of the primary surviving Stoic works. It's through his musings that we understand the Stoic mind. His thoughts are wide ranging, but we find someone who wrestles with his own thoughts, seeks practical wisdom, and, as emperor, yearns to understand justice. He also contemplates his life in light of the universe's immensity in both space and time. Marcus shows us that no matter a person's social standing, they can find Stoic harmony.

3

___

STOIC PHILOSOPHY

When people hear the word philosophy, often they think it's not for them or that it's impractical. In reality, stoicism is the most practical philosophy ever made. Entrepreneur Tim Ferriss says that it's a personal operating system for the mind. Stoicism is a fantastic operating system for thriving in high-stress environments. I think that's the main reason that people like Marcus Aurelius adopted stoicism. Even entrepreneurs, artists, and athletes today are still using stoicism 2,000 years later for one main reason: it can help you solve your problems.

Stoicism is the philosophy for you, and it's the philosophy for me, because it acts as an inner compass that will help us make decisions day by day. It will help us have this sense of equanimity and a sense of being the best man or the best woman that we can be. Stoicism has a direct impact on every decision that we make and every decision that we think. It is being used to remove anxiety and depression and getting people to stop procrastinating, become disciplined, and start taking action. Stoicism is the best philosophy if you actually want to directly impact your brain and have it work in the most optimal way possible.

Physics and Logic

There are three main components of stoic philosophy, but the two most important will be discussed here briefly. The first is physics, which refers to the way the world works and all of its natural processes. The second is logic, which in essence is rational thought. The two aspects work in tandem to describe the way stoics view the world—through a lens of logic applied to reality.

Both physics and logic, even in the context of philosophy, can get a little complex, so only the basics will be covered here. Stoic physics gave stoics the ground to stand on, so to speak, by defining and exploring what the universe is made of and why it behaves the way it does. These explanations and observations could then be used to shed light on situations common to the human condition. Rather than life being one big enigma, stoics aimed to bring a little sense to the disorder.

Logic works with this by explaining the universe in ways that line up with reason. Stoic logic was extraordinarily similar to the logic that we know, teach, and use today, such as in computer programming. For example, if this, then this. Logics essentially explains what things are like and why they're not any other way by defining aspects of the world and statements as true and false.

. . .

The third aspect of the philosophy that we won't dive too deep into is ethics. Stoics through the ages have argued about where exactly ethics fits within the framework and what importance it holds, but the general view is that ethics cannot exist without logic, because logic can tell you what is ethical and what is not.

Irrational Passions

As you can guess, irrational passions are voluntary responses, which are not positive aspects that stoics encourage. Irrational passions are also known as unhealthy or unnatural passions, indicating just how much the stoics felt they should be avoided. According to Zeno, unhappiness can be traced back to these irrational passions. There are many divisions and subdivisions of irrational passion, but what it all boils down to is the following:

- **Pain** - envy, resentment, sorrow, anxiety, confusion
- **Fear** - shame, panic, shock, dread, superstition
- **Craving** - want, sexual desire, need for wealth and material possessions.
- **Pleasure** - enchantment, spirited satisfaction

Stoics assert that these irrational passions lead to unhappiness. You might still be determining why pleasure is on this list, but stoics believe that an excess of many things, including pleasure, is detrimental. Excess pleasure can cause us to forsake logic, which is a big no-no in stoicism.

Good Passions

Just as there are irrational passions, there is another side of the coin, the good passions. These are, you guessed it, the ones you want. These good passions aren't virtues, per se, but they contribute to our happiness and ability to live virtuously. Keep in mind that the main thing separating good passions from the irrational is that good passions stem from a place of reason. There is logic behind their existence, which makes them natural while irrational passions are unnatural.

Good passions can be described as follows:

- Joy or delight (in place of pleasure)
- Caution or discretion (in place of fear)
- Wishing or willing (in place of craving)

All of these passions come from a place of logic and reason. Joy is a logical feeling stemming from something positive, caution is logical and necessary for self-preservation, and wishing is a natural human quality that is also logical because wishing and willing is how to discover what's important to us.

4

KEY PRINCIPLES OF STOICISM YOU NEED TO KNOW

Stoicism can be a lot to take in at first glance, but there are several guiding principles that can help guide you through some of the confusion that you may initially experience. For those unaccustomed to some of the terminology and rhetoric, Stoicism can seem quite alien. But the interesting thing is; once you get to the core of what Stoicism actually stood for, most in the Western world will find that the core principles of Stoicism are basically wrapped up in a universal code of conduct that has been practiced all over the world.

Just think of "practice makes perfect"—how many times have you heard of that? Well, it was a Stoic concept long before anyone else used it. And what about, "Everything in moderation"—where did that come from? Well, it's nothing short of one of the main virtues of stoic philosophy. Having that said, we are going to delve even deeper into such tried and true principles, so that we can make what might have been initially unfamiliar, much more familiar to you. So without further ado, here are the top 10 principles of Stoicism that you need to know.

Use Your Own Judgement

The number one principle for Stoics, is the principle of judgement. And no—it's not a clarion call to make it our personal mission to go around judging people. We certainly have enough of that in the world as it is! On the contrary, for Stoics having the right kind of judgement meant being able to appropriately respond in any given situation and even suspend our judgment if need be.

According to this principle, one of the ultimate goals of Stoicism is to learn to react to our own rational judgement rather than simply having a knee-jerk response to whatever comes our way. The Roman Emperor, turned Stoic philosopher Marcus Aurelius, perhaps said it best when he stated, "If any external thing causes you distress, it is not the thing itself that troubles you, but your own judgment about it. And this you have the power to eliminate now."

Perhaps American President Franklin Delano Roosevelt when addressing the nation during the Great Depression, was channeling Marcus Aurelius a bit when he declared, "There is nothing to fear but fear itself!" Because Marcus was saying much the same thing.

The basic takeaway from all this is that no matter what happens, we should not get so overwhelmed that we become a mindless reactionary to external events outside of our immediate control. If you accidentally rear-end a car in traffic for example, you shouldn't get out and start sobbing over what happened, instead you need to take proactive measures to make the situation better.

When you were a kid there's probably been occasions in which someone told you, "don't cry over spilled milk." Well, that's actually a very Stoic thing to say. In other words, what's done is done, you can't change external events that occur, but you can use your own mind, your own judgment, to rationally figure out the best way to move forward. Accord to Stoic philosophy, rather than just immediately reacting on impulse, we should go through three stages in response to any crisis.

In real time, it should go something like this; an incident occurs, we judge or size up the situation, and then we react. Do you see the difference? Instead of immediately reacting without thinking about the consequences, the Stoic takes time to consider the situation before responding. Having that said, of course, not all situations would give you much time for reflection.

If someone was coming at you with a baseball bat, for example, you just might have to default to regular old fight or flight.

Because if you stand there in deep thought and contemplation for too long while a bat-wielding maniac takes pot-shots at you, the consequences might not be too good. But having that said, in most other situations in life, you should be able to have enough time to judge the circumstances of an incident before you immediately react to it.

And where this principle of Stoicism really shines is in everyday, common interaction. Because there are plenty of times in which we interact with people, that we have bad reactions which may not be as visceral as the aforementioned bat-wielding assailant, but due to our own response can become just as devastating. Let's say for example you are in the breakroom at your workplace and you feel that one of your coworkers has slighted you.

It's certainly not a life or death situation, but it's unpleasant enough to provoke a severe reaction all the same. And many in the heat of the moment, will react without thinking, and say something that they may seriously regret later on. Such a situation presents the perfect time to employ the Stoic principle of judgment. Those with no judgement—let alone impulse control—might end up going off on their coworker in a profanity laced tirade.

What would be the result of all this? Most likely that employee would soon be looking for another line of work.

And what did they gain by their actions?

While standing in the unemployment line, they would most likely tell you—nothing at all. Having that said, if someone offends, instead of immediately reacting, you need to learn to step back from the situation, consider all of the factors involved, and then proceed with the most rational response in light of the circumstances.

In order to have a Stoic frame of mind, you need to avoid being prompted and prodded by external stimulus. Instead of having knee-jerk reactions to outside forces, you should be able to look within yourself for how you respond, and not be so easily malleable to outside factors. With good judgement we learn to make better use of our own mind rather than being influenced by the actions and opinions of others.

Just to drive this point home, let's return to the scenario of someone dealing with a coworker's slight in the workplace. If someone immediately reacts in anger or pain, it means the rudeness of their associate is of great importance to them. It's amazing sometimes how important we place the opinions of other people—even people we don't particularly care for— above our own.

By angrily responding to a colleague's rude remarks, you are actually giving them weight.

By placing importance on your coworker's critiques, you are making the judgement, whether intentionally or unintentionally, that the opinion of this person matters. Instead, you can step back, ponder the situation and come to the conclusion this troublesome individual's words mean nothing and their opinion is completely irrelevant.

.   .   .

It takes a strong mind with good judgement to be able to avoid being ensnared by outside agitators who seek to disturb you. The key thing to take away from this, is to realize we are in control of our actions and we can control how we react to whatever comes our way. In considering this, I can remember the words of my own father, who used to advise me along much the same lines, telling me, "You can't control others. The only one you can control is yourself."

I guess my old man was a Stoic and he didn't even know it, because that statement perfectly sums up what it means to abide by the Stoic principle of judgment. Having that said, it's amazing how out of control people are anymore. All you have to do is turn on the news—or better yet drive down the street! And you will see plenty of people having a very hard time controlling their own actions.

There are terrible cases of road rage each and every day where folks lose their mind over the smallest (or in some instances even imaginary) infractions of other motorists. In order to avoid this fate, we all need to step back and use our better judgment as much as we possibly can.

Even though we may all want to change the world—it's much easier to change ourselves first.

Because as this Stoic principle confirms, our experiences in life very much revolve around our own innate judgement. In

Stoicism, much of how we respond to any given situation is not so much generated by those around us as it is determined by what's inside of us. In other words, it's our own judgements (or lack thereof) that determines the outcomes of our interactions.

For those who are used to constantly reacting without thinking, learning to step back and make rational judgement might be challenging at first. It could seem like our reactions our second nature, and that we are unable to modify them. According to the Stoic Seneca, the reason such things are so difficult is quite frankly, because one who does not harness the will of their judgement has grown "soft."

Or as Seneca put it, "When pleasures have corrupted both mind and body, nothing seems to be tolerable—not because the suffering is hard, but because the sufferer is soft. For why are we thrown into a rage by somebody's cough or sneeze, by negligence in chasing a fly away, by a dog that gets in the way, or by the dropping of a key that has slipped from the hand of a careless servant?"

Going back to our road rage example used earlier, Seneca would probably judge that modern folks have become so soft and entitled that they fly into a rage over the pettiest of things.

It's because we've had it so good in the modern world, that we are often ready to fly off the handle over absolutely nothing at all.

. . .

In a world in which the nerves of many are in a constant state of heightened alert, it can be hard not to react outright. But the more you engage in these sorts of mental exercises, the more adept you will become at using your own judgement to rationally respond to any challenge you may face.

In order to put Stoic principles to practice you need to be able to suspend your judgement long enough to assess things as they come. When we do so, we often find that something we previously viewed as intolerable is not nearly as bad as it first seemed.

Perhaps the Stoic, Roman Emperor, Marcus Aurelius said it best when he declared, "Today I escaped from anxiety. Or no, I discarded it, because it was within me, in my own perceptions; not outside. Take away your opinion, and there is taken away the complaint. Take away the complaint, and the hurt is gone."

Don't Be Affected by Externals

As you may have already noticed, much of what the Stoics taught revolved around fine tuning our reactions to the external environment. As mentioned earlier, Stoicism teaches us to be careful how we judge the situations we find ourselves in, so we don't get tripped up by them, and start acting badly.

And in Stoic speak, an "external" is anything that is beyond our own purview that we normally have no direct control over. The goal of stoicism is to face these external factors head-on "without attachment." And this is the classic feature that sets Stoics apart—their utter refusal to let things that they cannot control, ruin their day. In other words, Stoics do not let external factors determine the mood they are in.

And you most especially do not let the opinions of others affect the opinion you hold of yourself. Of course, there is some nuance to this, and there certainly is some exception to the rule. The opinion of one's spouse for example, would naturally have a little more weight than the random stranger on the street. But even so, one's happiness cannot completely hinge even on one's spouse.

The Stoic must be strongly grounded in their own self-worth and not be affected by any externalities. Stoicism also stresses that it is important not to be deceived by an externality that seems frightening or enticing enough to compel us act. Stoicism teaches us to look at externals rationally, and resist the urge to think that we have influence over things we really do not.

Because while we can indeed control our own judgment/opinions of a situation, we have no control over external events and we furthermore need to make sure we are not mistakenly convinced we do.

The Stoic needs to be relatively unmoved by outside pressure that tries to convince one to intervene.

· · ·

Instead of being artificially affected and swayed one way or the other, the goal of the Stoic is to see things as they really are.

Or as Stoic philosopher Seneca described it, "So remember this above all, to strip away the disorder of things and to see what is in each of them; you will learn that nothing in them is frightening but the fear itself. What you see happening to boys, happens to us too. Their friends—the ones they are accustomed to and play with—if they see them wearing masks, they are terrified. The mask needs to be removed not just from people but from things, and the true appearance of each restored."

Seneca described irrational people to be like children who are startled when their playmates suddenly wear masks. According to Seneca, in a similar way, many of the outside externalities we face in this world, are not what they seem. And if we were to simply unmask them for what they are, our fears, anxieties, and perhaps even fascination, would quickly subside.

For a Stoic, it is absolutely imperative not to get overwhelmed by externalities, and instead keep things in perspective. Stoics therefore do not hedge their bets solely on snap judgement, but instead rely on their critical thinking ability to see matters clearly. In order to do so, Stoics teach to not project their own impressions on an external event. To illustrate this in action, take the following hypothetical as an example.

·   ·   ·

Let's say you are walking around at your local shopping mall and see a friend dining at a nearby food court. You look over at the person, expecting they might engage you. The person then looks up and briefly seems to make eye contact with you, but then quickly looks away. The sensitive person would most likely be offended. Their mind would start reeling with indignation as they proceed to project their most negative possible interpretation of the incident.

You think to yourself, "Did he just snub me? I know he saw me! What did I ever do to deserve being disrespected like that?" But these are all personal projections on an externality. In reality all you really know is that the person seemed to look at you and then for whatever reason, they looked away. Nothing more. Nothing less. But by projecting all of your anxieties and fears onto the event, suddenly the situation has become a major insult and affront, leaving you feeling as if you had just been treated terribly by someone who you thought was your friend.

These are all false creations of the observer however, and were artificially added to the externality. Now let's continue on with this scenario of the person who thought they were so rudely snubbed. Let's say the following week you bump into that person from the mall once again. Yet this time the reaction is much different. The friend walks right up, makes eye contact and has a big grin fills their face, they exclaim, "Hey man! Good to see you!"

Immediately you are in a quandary. Why are they so friendly all of the sudden? After they snubbed you like that at the mall? Shortly into the conversation however you find the answer, your best was not ignoring you after all, they had just undergone eye surgery, and had been having trouble making out faces from a distance. My, how the mask you put on that poorly judged externality, came falling right off! Now don't you feel silly?

And all of it was completely unnecessary in the first place. This faulty and detrimental understanding of external events, is precisely what the Stoic is trying to avoid. People often completely misinterpret events by adding their often mistaken first impressions onto them. Stoicism seeks to free us from this false narrative of our own creation. Stoics teach us to cast out our imaginations.

Curiously, this is yet another parallel with Christianity, and in particular, the Apostle Paul in the New Testament of the Christian Bible. Because when one reads 2nd Corinthians 10:5, which expresses the need for, "Casting down imaginations, and every high thing that exalteth itself against the knowledge of God, and bringing into captivity every thought to the obedience of Christ."

We can see that the similarity to Stoicism is quite uncanny. Yes, the Apostle Paul was indeed, basically saying the same exact thing as the Stoics!

He was advising not to project our ill-conceived "imaginations" onto external events!

. . .

And furthermore, to use knowledge and self-discipline to control our impulses!

The only difference is that Paul inserted God into the mix, whereas the stoics would simply have advised to cast down imagination that exalt (give false impressions) over knowledge (true discernment), and left it at that.

Paul may have added a religious tone to the message, but it's basically the same exact concept. For it is the Stoic belief that we should not give in to false impressions, imaginations, high-minded pretensions (every high thing that exalteth itself?) when attempting to assess external events.

The Stoic realizes that humanity has a propensity to seek and create all kinds of patterns in life. It's for this reason we look up and see faces in clouds, or even the fact that we draw lines between stars to create constellations. The point is—we naturally tend to connect the dots when there is nothing there. The funny thing is, all the while that we are doing this, we trick ourselves into thinking we are being rational.

Just like the example of the guy who thinks his friend snubbed him at the mall, we are taking bits and pieces of external data, putting them together, and trying to make sense of them. But as the aforementioned example demonstrates, the conclusions that we draw are often incredibly off base.

.   .   .

By nature, we are creatures who attempt to reason and make sense of our environment, but the Stoics knew full well that there were times that we might let our reasoning and speculation run amuck. The man who thought he was snubbed by his friend, reasoned that his friend looked right at him and then proceeded to look away. In his mind at the time, this was reason enough for him to conclude he had just been horribly insulted.

This is what he reasoned, but his reasoning or rationalizing of the external data he perceived was highly inaccurate. He of course had no way of knowing that his friend had just had eye surgery and the fact he couldn't see clear enough to recognize him, was the real reason that he looked away. The offended party didn't have this bit of crucial information so they let their mind go wild to connect dots that weren't there.

This is why Stoicism stresses to just see things exactly as they transpire and add nothing more, and nothing less. The Stoic would observe the same situation and simply report back that someone appeared to look at them and then looked away. There would be no dramatic conclusion that the action was a personal affront to the Stoic, merely that this was what had occurred.

Stoics choose not to overly exert themselves asking why things happen, they merely state the facts readily at hand and move on. The sooner you learn not to be affected by externals, the sooner you will be free from fruitless speculation. The embracing of this practice can be truly liberating for those who suffer from anxiety, since much of what we are anxious about are our own interpretations of the external environment. Take this principle to heart and you will not be troubled by such things anymore.

Keeping the Right Perspective

In Stoicism, there are two main methods of discernment that are typically employed. First, is the analytical method which entails suppressing our own snap judgments, and false impressions, so we can unmask externalities, and see them for what they are. The other method however, is an intuitive one that seeks to filter all experience through our own intuition in order to alter our perspective.

If you look at an issue from one angle, and then are simply able to shift your perspective, we are then able to remove ourselves from the equation so we can evaluate the situation in a state of detachment. The Stoics show us the mistake we make when we view our place in the universe, and our sense that we are somehow significant in the grand scheme of things.

Stoics contend that our inflated sense of ego is derived from our faulty perspective. By default, we tend to associate everything with how it relates to us and our situation. Things that occur during our finite life here on this planet seem like a big deal, but as the Stoics describe it, this is just a major misnomer on our part. The Stoic seeks to instill in us by our own intuition, how minuscule our petty concerns are when compared to the grand tapestry of creation.

. . .

These efforts are meant to make the budding Stoic a little humbler, and a virtuous life more appealing. Some might at first feel that looking upon human life as minuscule and often times, rather meaningless, would be a reason for depression. But on the contrary, Stoics, felt it was freeing and reassuring instead.

And the humbleness that such shifts in perspective bring about are rewarding for their ability to cure us of any lingering avarice, envy, strife, or misplaced priorities. By shifting the focus away from ourselves, it helps us to better look toward the greater good of humanity/existence.

Stoicism existed as a powerful movement from approximately 200 BC to 200 AD, and it's interesting to note that out of all the philosophies prevalent some 2,000 odd years ago, Stoicism was unique in its sense that humanity was insignificant.

At a time when most other belief systems had man as the center of the universe, with the sun, moon, planets, and stars literally revolving around the Earth—the Stoics held that man's place in the cosmos was as more of a sideshow, rather than being anywhere near center stage.

The Roman Emperor and esteemed Stoic philosopher, Marcus Aurelius perhaps summed it up best when he wrote, "Asia and Europe are corners of the universe; the whole of the sea is a drop in the universe; Athos, a tiny clod of dirt in the universe; all the present time is one point in eternity. Everything is small, easily changing; disappearing."

Marcus Aurelius was able to describe all the oceans of the planet as just a drop in the universe. This he managed to do thousands of years before space exploration enabled the likes of the famed astronomer Carl Sagan to come to much the same conclusion when he presented our whole entire planet as nothing more than a "pale blue dot suspended in a sunbeam."

It was on Valentine's Day, February 14th, 1990, when NASA's Voyager spacecraft soaring toward the edge of the solar system, famously looked back, and took a snapshot of the Earth from nearly 4 billion miles away. The image of the planet which took up less than a pixel in the photo, revealed, as Carl Sagan put it, that, "the Earth is a very small stage in a vast cosmic arena."

As Sagan rightly described, seeing the Earth, the entire sum total of human history and aspiration presented as nothing more than a minuscule dot in the vacuum of space does much to change your perspective of things. But the Stoics didn't need NASA to tell them this. They already intuitively knew it! And the fact that an ancient Stoic could have such a powerful sense of perspective is rather remarkable.

Perhaps Mr. Sagan was inspired by Marcus in the first place, because as one continues to read through Marcus Aurelius' meditations, you can find yet another chief example of this

Stoic perspective that strikes an even more similar sounding refrain.

Because it was Marcus Aurelius who had declared, "The Earth with its cities and peoples, its rivers and encircling sea, if measured by the universe, we may regard as a mere dot. Our life occupies a portion smaller than a dot, if it is compared with all of time, because the measure of eternity is greater than that of the world; the world recreates itself over and over within the bounds of time." Less than a pixel, smaller than a dot, however you look at it—one's perspective is forever changed in the knowledge of how finite our world really is.

Reigning in Desire/Passion

One of the main, prevailing themes of Stoicism is that unhappiness is the result of how we perceive/judge our hopes and concerns for tomorrow, in relation to the joy and sorrow of today. In order to better navigate through this potential minefield, the Stoic must learn how to use logical reasoning.

And it stands to reason, that most of us tend to want things that we don't have. Whether it's that job promotion that's out of reach, that luxurious mansion up on the hill, or whatever the case may be—us human beings tend to yearn for the things that we lack rather than counting on all the blessing we currently have at our disposal. The Stoic's argue however, that the idea that we even want any of these things is a false narrative we have created.

. . .

And in reality, it's not that we want these bigger and better things, it's that we think we want them. Because most of the time when people acquire something they yearn for, they're not satisfied, and it's not long before they start looking for something else. So, keeping this in mind, it's the Stoics who contend that what really drives most of us is the pursuit of goals and objects we think will make us happy, rather than the end result itself.

In other words, we are enamored with the thrill of the chase, but by the time we corner our prize, like a cat bored with a caught mouse, we're ready to cast it to the side. This is why highly successful people, millionaires and billionaires and the like, are often some of the most miserable individuals you could ever meet. They've been to the top of the mountain and have become bored with the view. That object we so yearned for, is now repugnant to us at worst, and absolutely meaningless at best.

Stoics called this lack of satisfaction, the "insatiability of desires." According to Stoicism, our desires are insatiable. We are never satisfied. The more things we acquire in life, the more we feel like we lack. We keep wanting bigger and better things. What we have is never enough. Like an addict in need of a fix, sometimes success itself can be a drug with the individual driven to reach a high mark that seems to get higher each and every achievement they make.

This is why for a Stoic the reining in of our desires/passion is so important. In later stoicism much emphasis is placed on this, and inflamed passion is even likened to a being a "disease" that needs to be eradicated. Stoic leader, Chrysippus was a definite proponent of this, charging that continually giving way to one's passion would lead to a "diseased state of mind" in which a perpetual false narrative is created.

It was perhaps the Stoic philosopher Epictetus who said it best when he declared, "Don't you know how thirst works in someone with a fever? It is nothing like the thirst of a man in good health. He drinks and is no longer thirsty. The sick man is happy only for a moment, then is nauseous; he converts the drink into bile, he vomits, his stomach hurts, and then he is thirstier still. It is just like this to crave riches and have riches, to crave power and have power, to crave a beautiful woman and sleep with her."

In order to escape the endless cycle of pursuit that Epictetus describes, one must gain control of their impulses and blunt their desires, lest they be overtaken by them completely.

Learning to Live in the Present

Stoicism teaches a form of mindfulness, that seeks to have its adherents live in the present rather than dwelling on the past or fearing the future. Stoics would remind their pupils that what's done is done—you can't go back in time to correct mistakes of the past. Likewise, you can't jump ahead and know the future.

Therefore, it was consistently taught that one should do their best to live in the present. For a Stoic who practiced living in the present, each new day was basically a "reset" on their whole existence.

There was no sadness over what happened yesterday or dread over what may happen tomorrow, stoics simply lived in the now and took things as they came.

You might recall from earlier in this book when we mentioned the example of Cato the Younger. Cato was attacked by a man in a Roman bathhouse. The next day however, he completely put it out of his mind. So much so, that when his assailant even apologized for the previous day's actions, Cato claimed he didn't even remember it. Choosing to forget the past, Cato was living for the present.

The Stoic must dispel any lingering doubts about the past or fear of the future. As Seneca put it, "Two things we must therefore root out: fear of distress in the future and the memory of distress in the past. The one concerns me no longer. The other concerns me not yet." In other words, the past is over, so why worry about it? And at the same time the future hasn't happened yet, so there is no need fretting over future events.

Instead of getting ahead in life, many of us feel as if we are stuck on a treadmill, always struggling to keep up. We look back at the past and feel that we haven't accomplished enough, and yet we dread the future, fearing that our efforts will fall short. The Stoic however, breaks this cycle by living in the moment, and refusing to entertain doubts of the past, or fears of the future either one. The Stoic simply keeps putting one foot in front of the other, and takes life as it comes.

Not Being Overcome by Emotion

Even though Stoics carry the well-known stereotype of "being stoic"—Stoicism is not as devoid of emotion as people think. In fact, stoicism encourages emotion. It just needs to be used in a productive fashion. Because as Stoic philosopher Seneca explained it, "I should not be unfeeling like a statue; I should care for my relationships both natural and acquired—as a pious man, a son, a brother, a father, [and] a citizen."

So just what kind of emotive expression do the Stoic philosophers recommend? Emotions should only be expressed so much as they don't disrupt our ability to think rationally. As a rule, the Stoics determine whether or not their emotion exceeds its bounds, by virtue of how much they disturb our internal equilibrium. If, for example, someone is extremely upset about an issue, they will most likely have trouble making logical decisions.

And likewise, if someone is so enamored with an externality that it affects their decision-making process, their judgement on that matter should not be trusted.

Any overwhelming emotion that could be perceived as a threat to sound judgment should be avoided. Having that said, Stoics acknowledged there were some cases—despite how one might try—in which not being overcome by emotions might indeed be hard thing to do.

Or as Seneca famously put it, when discussing this matter with a colleague of his, "There are certain things, Lucilius, that no courage can avoid; nature reminds courage of its own mortality. And so, the courageous man will frown at sad things; he will be startled by a sudden occurrence; he will feel dizzy if, standing at the brink, he looks down from the precipice. This is not fear but a natural feeling not to be overcome by reason."

We are only human after all, and if placed in a shocking enough circumstance even the best of Stoics could be caught off guard. Seneca expounded upon this further by describing such instances as merely a "momentary lapse of reason." Seneca stated, "An emotion, then does not consist in being moved by the appearances of things but in surrendering to them and following up this casual impulse. For if anyone supposes that turning pale, bursting into tears, sexual arousal, deep sighs, flashing eyes, and anything of that sort are a sign of emotion and mental state, he is mistaken and does not understand that these things are merely bodily impulses. A man thinks himself injured, wants to be revenged, and then being dissuaded for some reason—he quickly calms down again. I don't call this anger, but a mental impulse yielding to reason."

For the Stoic, having firm control of our emotional drives is of the utmost importance. Many are unduly blinded by their emotions and provoked to respond in ways that might not be in their best interest. We need to be in the driver's seat at all times in order to avoid impulsive behavior.

Having that said however, even the Stoics recognized that there are occasions in which controlling one's emotions would be harder than others. If for example, you just received word one of your loved ones had passed away, even a Stoic wouldn't begrudge you for bursting into tears. Seneca for one, accepted such things as a natural consequence of human nature.

The difference between how a Stoic and a non-Stoic handles such things however is a Stoic makes sure not to wallow in grief, as soon as the natural wave of emotion passes over, the Stoic returns to a state of reason, refraining from being overcome any further by emotional excess.

Overcoming Fear of Death

In Stoic philosophy, death is the ultimate external event. Short of suicide, we have no way to naturally control when we die. As such, death is usually viewed with fear. Since Stoic philosophy seeks to alleviate such feelings with reason, it is no wonder they would spend considerable time and energy seeking to overcome the fear of death.

In contemplation of death Stoics reason that the most frightening part of death for most, is simply the mystery involved in it.

. . .

But having that said, the actual end result, according to the Stoics, "leaves us no worse off than we were before we were born." Stoics furthermore contend that death is a "continuous" and "natural" process that takes place over the course of one's life.

Death therefore, should be feared no more than birth, or any other natural part of existence in this world. Stoics believed that fear of death was due to lack of reason, and overcoming this fear with rational analysis was a liberating experience. But much more than just seeking to free the adherent from their fear of death, Stoics taught their pupils that death was a great agent for gaining insight and even encouragement. As the Stoics saw it, "mortality is the defining feature of our existence."

We are indeed here for a short time. Just the very thought of how finite our life is, brings new perspective and meaning to what we should be doing during our brief period of existence. It is for this reason that Stoics were known to "meditate on death" in order to produce certain virtues such as humbleness, courage, and temperance. The Stoics sought to unmask death, and see it for what it truly was—simply a natural result of life.

According to Stoicism, despite the fear that the notion of death generates, death was not necessarily a bad thing in itself.

. . .

Or as Seneca described it, "Death belongs among those things that are not evils in truth, but still have an appearance of evil; for a love of self is implanted in us, and a desire of existence and survival, and a dread of disintegration.

Death seems to rob us of many good things and to remove us from all we have come to know. And there is another element that estranges us from death we are already familiar with the present, but are ignorant of the future into which we will go, and we shrink from the unknown. Even if death is something indifferent, then it is nevertheless a thing that cannot be easily ignored."

As Seneca acknowledged, death is not easy to dismiss, but as the Stoics taught, with concerted concentration, we can work to overcome much of our fear of death and dying. And perhaps it was Seneca who said it best when he declared, "What is death? A mask to frighten children. Turn it and examine it. See, it does not bite. The poor body must be separated from the spirit as it was before, either now or later. Why then are you troubled if it be now?"

As has been mentioned a few times in this book, there are striking similarities between Stoic perspectives and early Christianity. Seneca's take on death provides us with another one, since the Apostle Paul clearly seconded his opinion when in the Book of 1st Corinthians, he too declared, "Death! Where is thy sting!" The concept of death takes up much thought in the world of the living, but the sooner we unmask it, much of that initial sting—the fear of death—does indeed go out of it.

. . .

The Stoics of antiquity themselves, lived in a very uncertain world.

The average lifespan was much shorter than what we enjoy today and the chance of dying from injury or disease was much greater. As such, the Stoics felt it rather expedient to teach their followers to lose their fear of death early on. By ridding themselves of this ever-present facet of their external environment they could then free themselves to pursue life in its fullest.

Dealing with Adversity

Just like everyone else, Stoics do not look forward to adversity. Unnecessary hardship is certainly not something that they actively seek out. Nevertheless, when adversity does come their way, they strive to prevent themselves from becoming overly affected by it. On the contrary, despite any difficulty, for a Stoic, adversity is seen as a potential opportunity in which they can use adversity to improve their disposition.

Stoics view hard times as a kind of proving ground, like the fires in a forge which help to shape and mold them into a stronger, better person. In this Stoics are seeking to find inherent benefit, even in what might initially appear to be undesirable situations. The stoics view adversity in the same way that they view death. They view it as an often-misunderstood external factor, that if harnessed appropriately, could be used for good.

. . .

Stoics contend that something is a hardship for us, simply because we perceive it that way. But if we would just suspend our judgement and step back for a moment, we just might see that what we are facing was not as bad as it may have appeared at first glance. And what's more, there may even be some intrinsic good in what previously appeared to be entirely bad.

Once again, it all boils down to the basic Stoic teaching that even though we have no control over many external events, we can indeed control how we respond to them. As such, whenever hardship arises, the Stoic attempts to make it into a teaching moment, in order to better themselves. Also, since Stoicism advises that our first impressions are often mistaken, a slow approach to analyzing a hardship is used, in case it turns out to be a true blessing in disguise.

When faced with certain kinds of adversity, Stoics will also often try to put themselves into the shoes of others, and shift their perspective enough to see the situation differently. With these changes in perspective, the hardship often does not appear as bad at first glance.

Stoic Philosopher Seneca described as much, when he said, "Do you think that the wise man is burdened by evils? He makes use of them.

. . .

It was not only from ivory that Phidias knew how to make statues; he made them also from bronze.

If you had given him marble, or some still lesser material, he would have carved the best statue that could be made of it.

So the wise man will display virtue amid riches if possible, but if not, in poverty; at home if he can, but if not, in exile; as a general if he can, but if not, as a solder; in sound health if he can, but if not, then in weakness. Whatever fortune he is dealt, he will make of it something remarkable."

Yes, according to the Stoics, adversity is truly what you make of it. If you feel that the hardships are insurmountable, they will remain so. But if you look toward them as redefining moments, you can learn to adjust. And the sooner you do, the more successful you will be. As soon as any adversity emerges, instead of shrinking away from the challenge, you should face it head-on.

Don't be Blinded by Greed and Pleasure

Much of Stoic doctrine speaks at length over how we can learn to control both our perceptions and our impulses, desires, and passions. All human beings of course desire the good things in life, but the Stoics issue stern warnings for those who would be consumed by gluttony and greed.

According to Stoicism, anything that a man may have unchecked avarice for, he could later become ensnared by.

The Stoics caution their followers to not be so blinded by the greed of this world that they lose sight of what's important. According to this principle of Stoicism, greed, and the love of riches has the propensity to create quite a bit of strife in our lives.

The Stoics contend that greed usually follows a typical pattern. Someone obtains things that they greatly value, but are not satisfied. Instead they immediately have fear and doubt should they lose their precious commodity. Not only that, they are also desirous of more of it, never satiated with what they actually have.

As well as being applicable to material riches, the same thing could be applied to any perceived pleasure in life. There are countless people out there who are addicted to physical and emotional pleasures and these addictions more or less follow the same patterns that the Stoics outlined. Just look at any given addiction; whether it be drugs, alcohol, food, gambling, or even relationships.

They all can succumb to this unhealthy cycle of desire, fear of loss, and yearning for more of the same. Just take the example of a domineering, abusive husband. At first glance one might think such a person hates their wife, due to the way they treat them. But in reality, that person greatly values their spouse like a prized commodity, and therefore seeks to obsessively control everything they do.

. . .

This person has an irrational fear of losing their spouse, so they seek to dominate them entirely. At the same time the domineering husband might also have a wandering eye and cultivate other relationships elsewhere, because despite their tyrannical hold on their own spouse, deep down they are not satisfied and yearn for further fulfillment.

In order to remedy such a situation, the Stoic would once again stress moderation. Stoics recommend a slight detachment from the things we desire, in order to prevent greed. We need to resist chasing after rewards, and refrain from clinging from them once we have them. And we need to strengthen our resolve not to become completely devastated if we were to lose them, as this is an externality and all externals are ultimately uncertain in the end.

Seneca perhaps summed this sentiment up best when he remarked, "He who has need of riches feels fear on their account. But no man enjoys a blessing that brings anxiety. He is always trying to add a little more. While he puzzles over increasing his wealth, he forgets how to use it."

We need to learn to appreciate what's in our hand and not seek out more than we actually need. Marcus Aurelius was probably one of the best experts on this Stoic Mindset since he was the all-powerful ruler of the Roman Empire. One can only imagine the wealth and excess that most have been at his disposal. Yet, Marcus was one was always sure to keep any propensity for greed in check.

. . .

Even though he could have lived a lavish life he usually opted for austerity. Instead of wearing expensive clothes, he wore the most basic of tunics. Rather than be a glutton for fine wine and expensive food, he only consumed what was necessary. Marcus Aurelius knew full well how to avoid being blinded by greed and excess pleasure, and the modern Stoic would do well to follow his example.

Don't Worry About What Others Think

For Stoics, it is very important to learn how to avoid being affected by the outside world. And a major part of this is through not worrying too much over what others might think. Stoics realize that we all seek approval from others in various ways, but Stoicism calls for us to avoid such "vanity and pride."

Stoics identify such things as yearning for recognition by externals; friends, family, and the like. We all want to be accepted, but Stoicism teaches us to have "contempt for conformity."

Never mind what everyone else thinks, the Stoic only does what they themselves believes to be right. Sadly, most people do not fall into this category. Most do indeed live by a certain amount of groupthink; the dangerous excesses of which have been seen all throughout history.

Just think of any atrocity committed in the past few centuries and you will find that every day, average people did awful things just to conform with what others in society were doing.

Everyone else was doing it, so they felt that either it must be right, or they had simply no choice but to conform, lest they stand out and become targets themselves. Go to any war crimes trial and you will no doubt hear more than one person make the claim that they were simply, "following orders."

Stoics completely reject the idea that human beings are social lemmings who have to follow what others are doing. Stoics acknowledge however, that breaking away from the pack can be difficult. And that the prevailing opinions of any given society often does pressure the individual to conform. But Stoicism calls for resistance all the same. In order to do this, Stoics call for their followers to not have an "appetite for praise" since it is in seeking the accolades of others that we become lackeys to social directives.

Instead of seeking approval from others, the Stoic has to stop and ask, "Why do I care if they like what I'm doing or not?" For a Stoic it is natural to develop skepticism of prevailing public opinion. Stoics are fully aware most people fail to use their own critical thinking and are easily swayed by public pressure. As such, public consensus does not hold much weight with them.

Instead Stoics argue that it is better to trust one's own judgment and not worry about what others may think as a consequence. The Stoic uses their own mind to decide what is right and their decisions are not based on the desires of others.

As none other than a Roman Emperor named Marcus Aurelius put it, "The part of the good man is not to peer into the character of others, but to run straight down the line without glancing one side or the other." The Stoic needs to be a straight shooter, know their own convictions and do what's right—no matter what anyone else might think about it.

5

THE STOIC LOGIC

Stoicism is a philosophy that I've been living and practicing for quite some time. It is really important to know about how Stoics react to specific unfortunate and uncomfortable events. This could be the death of a family member, losing your job, getting dumped by your partner, or even something as tiny as going grocery shopping while you're angry. Stoicism follows the belief that practicing specific virtues, such as wisdom, results in long-term happiness.

Furthermore, stoicism is a very practical philosophy because it is based on the belief that we cannot control external events or our circumstances. Yet stoics have the power to react to these events in a specific manner. Stoics are able to objectively react and cope with the struggles of life. They pursue objectivity and logical reasoning instead of impulsiveness and giving in to our inner urges.

. . .

Stoicism is about accepting that we are on this planet for a short duration. We have to realize that not only we ourselves are short-lived, but also everything that we experience in our lifetime. In my opinion, stoicism is one of the best if not the best approach to getting more out of life. It is rational, and it is especially beneficial for people who strive for improvement, as it focuses on controlling immediate urges like food cravings or addiction. It is therefore not only beneficial for our careers, but also for our health.

Unfortunate life events, as already mentioned, could be losing a loved one, losing your job, losing your house, not getting a job, failing an exam, or pretty much anything that seems really really unpleasant. Most people will be either pissed off or sink into a deep hole of self-pity. For example, we could be mad because our boss is not realizing how qualified we actually are. We could be angry because our teacher did not tell us about all the material that was required for the class. We could sink into self-pity because our girlfriend broke up with us. Lastly, we could even sink into a deep depression because we lost a sibling, a parent, or another much-appreciated person.

Whatever it may be, all of these reactions are by no means stoic. Instead, these are quite the opposite. They are an emotional, uncontrolled, and impulsive reaction to circumstances. A better explanation is this - it is simply not in our hands, or it is neither changing the situation in itself nor making us happier or benefiting us. I'm not saying we shouldn't feel grieved because we've lost someone. That's probably not possible for most people. Yet, we can control ourselves at least.

. . .

Imagine one of your friends going through one of these struggles. Either he lost someone, or he didn't get a job, or he didn't pass his exam. What would be your advice, or what would you tell him to do instead of increasing his negative feelings? Would you say yes, you deserved to fail that exam? You would probably encourage them, tell them we learn through our failures, it's just an exam, you can retake it easily, and next time you'll be prepared and then you're going to ace it. Or if he just got dumped by his girlfriend, you would probably not mention how ugly he is. Neither would you say that he's a jerk and he should have paid more attention to his relationship.

Instead, you would probably suggest that he move on. After all, they are plenty of fish in the sea. It is only one woman that dumped him, and there are so many more out there. Plus, she didn't deserve him in the first place. You might finish up with a phrase like, "That's just how life is. Nothing lasts forever."

We can clearly understand both sides, as we understand impulsive behavior, grief, and sadness, but we also understand the motivating side. So, the shift we want to make is to go from sadness and grief to the more objective and motivating view. We are in an unfortunate situation, but instead of impulsively reacting, we take a step back. We take an objective view. We give ourselves the same advice and we act in the exact same way that we would suggest someone else act. This can be quite hard, because we are frequently overruled by our emotions. Nevertheless, it is possible to remain objective, reasonable, and logical.

As a result, we will be able to control our own emotions better than our own reactions. We just need to reflect on the situation and understand that our reaction is our own doing. And yes, this is way easier said than done. Try reflecting on your situation. If you just got dumped, it's insanely hard to be a good friend to yourself, and following the advice given earlier is by no means easy. Yet if we practice this approach for all negative events, then we will eventually get better at it. After tediously working on controlling our emotions, we will eventually remain more rational when an unfortunate event strikes us. By being objective, we will not only minimize the feelings of sadness, anger, and hate, we also make the right decisions.

We won't be shouting at our spouse because we lost our job or we won't be losing our job because we fell into a deep depression after our mom died. We managed to keep it all under control. These gigantic events are fairly rare, and practicing them is beneficial but not really easy. Therefore, we have to practice self-control in our everyday life. We face hundreds of decisions each day, and we can train our self-control by not giving in to the bad decisions. We increase our strength by not giving in to our urges. We buy a salad instead of steak. We exercise instead of popping in another movie. We get up early instead of sleeping in.

In a nutshell, stoicism is a practical approach to living a better life. Stoics believed that they cannot control all of their circumstances, but they can control their reaction. Being rational is a quintessential part of stoicism, and this means that we should practice self-control, resist our immediate urges, and fight impulsive behavior, as these will only bring us into a downward spiral.

6

STOICISM AND HAPPINESS

D o you realize that at the end of the day, we really only have control over one thing? We don't have control over the weather, over the actions of other people, or on our genetics, nor over our past. None of that! But we can control our minds. We can't control the external, but we can control our thoughts and with our thoughts, we can influence our emotions and control our actions. Even that alone can be extremely powerful.

The key here with stoicism is to keep in mind that there is the only thing that we can control. Most people go through similar kind of things their entire lives and they go around thinking or not even thinking. They just kind of go around through their daily lives as if they have control over everything or rather worrying about everything external. They worry about the opinions of others, they worry about what the weather is going to be like, they worry about this or that, or they blame their genetics or their past or where they were born.

. . .

But the thing is, stoics realize that the only thing that we really can control is our minds. With that realization, the only thing that's really worth even focusing on or putting our time and energy into is optimizing our thoughts and having a high-quality mindset. That will lead to a life and a lifestyle that can breed peace of mind, happiness, and confidence. We have to keep in mind that what we need to do on a daily routine is to realize that. We shouldn't focus on or worry about anything outside of our control. So the next time something happens to you that's outside of your control, whether it's the weather, bad luck, or whatever it is, just keep in mind that the thing was bound to happen.

How you react to the situation really defines your character, and really will end up boiling down to more confidence for you. So if you do get into a car crash, or if something bad happens to you, remember how you have to respond to the situation. If you stay cool, calm, and calculated in that situation and you don't really stress about it, you don't really worry, and you still focus on the other good things that are going to come to you throughout your day, then afterward you know it's going to actually be easier for you to continue to focus on your thoughts and on your mind.

Stoicism and Happiness

Through stoicism, you are going to learn the exact method to raise your default level of happiness. I'm not talking about happiness from external objects like money or fame or anything like that. I'm talking about increasing your level of joy so you have this deep-rooted fulfillment that gives you pleasure at every moment of life, regardless of what your external circumstances are. Let us start with a quote from Seneca, who was a great philosopher back 2,000 years ago. According to him, true happiness is all about enjoying the present moment.

Someone who is not anxious about the future is also happier on the inside. Seneca said that someone who can be satisfied with what he already has is the real human. A human who has every contentment inside him. True happiness can be experienced by avoiding being anxious and without depending on the future. Seneca has told us so many things about being happy.

But don't get confused and think that Seneca is telling us that we shouldn't better ourselves or shouldn't aspire to gain material possessions in this world. This isn't the case, because Seneca himself was a very wealthy man. What he is telling us is actually an admonition against the lack of presence. People tend to forget about the present moment. We're always looking into the future and we're always looking into the past. We're always wishing for things, trying to get the next best thing and are never content with our lot. We suffer from the monkey mind, the distracted mind that lacks focus.

Of course, this is part of the human condition, and this is part of the social narrative. We are always thinking ahead, thinking of the family, our jobs, something we want to buy, or retirement. But the trap is that we miss out on living. We miss out on the present moment. Happiness is now. I really don't want you to get confused by this quote, thinking that Seneca is advising us not to want external things like money or happiness from external objects. If Seneca won the lottery, of course, he'd accept it. Seneca was a very wealthy man, so naturally he wouldn't advocate for less.

That's not the point. Instead, the point is to be content with what you have before you start looking for external things. To increase your happiness, Seneca is advising us to be completely present in the moment, stop thinking about the past, and stop thinking about the future. Neither of those things is real, because in the future that moment in time will be the present moment. You can't change the past, for it's done, and you can't change the future because it hasn't happened yet. All you have is the present moment, so live now in this present moment. Get into the present moment, and be aware of your surroundings.

Be aware that you're sitting down. Feel the scene, whether you are sitting on the bed or a couch or a chair. Sit and just be in the present moment. Take this time now to enjoy what you have. Stop thinking about the past, stop worrying about the future, and just be present right now. Whilst reading this book, appreciate that you have this time alone and that you have your computer or phone or wherever screen you're using. Just be completely present.

What happens over time is, our monkey mind gets completely distracted. It's only within our brain that we get an increase in happiness from external objects. Say, for example, you win the lottery and after some time your happiness increases a little bit. But after a week or a month or a year, your happiness goes back down to the default level. This is called the hedonic treadmill in science, and it states that whenever an external event happens to you, your happiness changes for a little bit. Whether it be a positive change or a negative change, after time you return to the default level of happiness.

This is just human nature, and this is what happens. This is why so many lottery winners enjoy the money for a certain length of time. After a while, their expectations increase, which brings the default level of happiness back down to where they were before they won the lottery. It's exactly the same thing if something negative happens. Say something is stolen from you. For a while you're annoyed at yourself, thinking why did I let this happen? But then, as time goes on, you return to your default level of happiness.

The advice that Seneca is giving you is to increase that level of happiness. To stop fluctuating between happiness and negative raises the bar completely. So, you can be completely content and completely joyful at all times. Let's reflect back. Think of when you were younger and you wanted something, like a toy. Now, let's say this thing you wanted it was an Xbox One, the first Xbox. When you were younger, you probably thought that this thing would bring you lots of happiness. You had dreams about it, you talked about it, and you begged your parents to buy it for you. If you were lucky, perhaps your parents did give in and they bought you the Xbox.

.   .   .

For the first few weeks or so, you were ecstatic. You were very happy, and you had heaps of joy as you played this thing. You played it until the gimmick wore off. What naturally happened is you started growing tired of it, so the happiness faded and you wanted something more. You wanted something else to rekindle that excitement. So the next thing you go for is maybe the Xbox 360, or a new bike, or maybe a new laptop, and so begins the cycle. Let me tell you a quick story that will help you internalize this point.

A few years ago, I wanted a new laptop. I dreamt about. I was obsessed with the idea, and I saved money from time to time, convincing myself that when I got this laptop I would be happy. I'd be completely content. So I got the laptop, and I was right! I was happy and I was completely content for a week, maybe. Then after a week, I got bored of the laptop and I wanted something better. This is the hedonic treadmill. My happiness level increased, but then it went back to the default level of happiness.

Now, this cycle doesn't end during childhood. It continues to adulthood. We are always looking for new job positions, new cars, new material things, new positions, or all of the above. But at the end of the day, we end up going back to a base level of happiness. Why are we never able to truly be content or fulfilled? Because there is always something else. It never ends.

If you were to lose your house right now and start living on the streets, of course you might be depressed to begin with. You might actually be suicidal for a while, but after a few months, maybe a year or two, your base level of happiness goes back to where it was. You adapt to the situation.

If you were to become a multimillionaire right now, you'd be pretty happy and you'd have a lot of time to enjoy yourself, but after a few years, once again, your base level of happiness returns to its normal level. This is why people are so surprised when they see celebrities that get depressed or commit suicide. This is what people don't understand about the hedonic adaptation. Material things don't matter.

After a while, things change, but happiness comes from within and it comes from paying attention to the present moment and enjoying it without really needing anything more. Once again, this doesn't necessarily mean that you shouldn't aspire for great things, but it means that you should be able to take some time to reflect, sit down, and enjoy the present moment.

Think of ways that this has happened in your life, and I promise you will find some resemblance to this situation. Then, remind yourself that you can stop looking for external things to increase your level of happiness, because happiness comes from within. I urge you to understand that happiness resides within yourself. You have happiness inside of your body. Just realize that, and you will be joyful, I promise.

How Happiness Feels To A Stoic

I'm going to guess that you've already read multiple articles and have gone through multiple books about happiness, and yet your happiness hasn't multiplied. Why is that? Listening and reading aren't the same as doing. All behavior, and all changes, must be trained. Stoics didn't write their material solely to be read. They created practical exercises in order to train your mind to respond properly to life so that you could live it well. Stoicism isn't concerned with difficult sayings and philosophies. Its focus is on helping us overcome harmful feelings and work on the things that can be changed.

Simply put, here are the Stoics most important exercises for happiness:

Get rid of your obstacles

This exercise is very powerful, because if you can properly fight your obstacles and get rid of them, you can become happy. Every bad becomes a potential source of good to the stoic. Everything is an opportunity. For example, situations where your hard work is underpaid or the demise or loss of a loved one occurs are not considered opportunities, generally. In fact, they can make you weak because they are obstacles. What do the stoic do? They believe there is a lesson to be learned in each and every experience we have in life, and that every obstacle that comes our way leads to more growth.

Rather than sulking or complaining, stoics ask themselves, "What have I learned from this experience?" and "How have I become a better person?" These are empowering questions. Most of us are not completely immune to external events or the bad things that happen to us. These result in bad feelings within us. However, recognizing that our lives still go on and we can't pity our situations is an outlook that can give us a completely different way of living. More importantly, this outlook can make us strong in adverse situations.

Is this within my control?

One of the most important practices in stoic philosophy is differentiating between what we can change and what we can't. Let's say a flight was delayed because of the weather, and no amount of arguing with the airline representative will end the bad weather. In another example, physically we may be taller or shorter than we want, but no amount of wishing will change that. What's important to realize is the time spent mulling over these unchangeable situations is often wasted. Don't fight the battles you can't win. When you realize that you can't control certain things, you feel happier.

Appreciate the present

Chasing future happiness is self-defeating. We can find happiness by accepting the present. If you refuse to accept your reality and always hope that you deserve a better future, this can result in robbing yourselves and present happiness. By seeing happiness as an outcome of some future achievements such as getting a certain job, more money, or finding a spouse, we start to lose sight of what we already have as our happiness right in this very moment. And even worse the plans for the future happiness do not go as desired. We will grow depressed similar to chasing future happiness. The

Stoics believe that developing a constant desire for one thing after another can be a reason to unhappiness. So they implanted the idea of accepting and gratifying things that are already there. By doing so, you can find ultimate satisfaction in whatever you have.

7

OLD STOICISM VS. MODERN STOICISM

Since we are human, we try to control as many things as possible to free ourselves from feelings of vulnerability and confusion to ultimately find happiness. To be able to deal with such situations, you can look to stoicism. Stoicism is an ancient philosophy which can be a great help with controlling thoughts.

Early stoicism was just based on how you can control yourself. It worked for some of the greatest emperors and kings. You can even argue that its ideas are more important than ever in this day and age because of social media. It is an aid in the popular movement of self-improvement. Writers like Tim Ferris and Robert Greene have written about stoicism and increased its popularity. People look to follow the teachings of stoicism to find calmness, peace within, and to better deal with all the chaos around them.

. . .

To better understand stoicism, we will look at the life and writings of Marcus Aurelius. Marcus Aurelius was a Roman emperor who had absolute power. He had a powerful army that was feared, he could have any woman he wanted, and he could have chosen to just have fun for the rest of his life. Momentary pleasure was available to him without limits.

But unlike some people who are corrupted by power, Marcus was different. He wrote about his struggles within himself in the now famous *Meditations*. Stoics observed that there are things not in our control, and most of these things are outside our mind. On the other side of this, there are things in our control, which are our internal thoughts, interpretations, and reactions. Reality does not care about our opinions, nor can we will it to, but it doesn't mean we are helpless victims of the world.

Most things are simply not up to us, like the attitudes of our colleagues or how the economy is doing, and there is nothing we can do to exclude misfortune. What is under our control are our opinions, actions, and how we interpret the world around us. Stoics focus on the things they can control. When we believe that things outside ourselves or things in the future will bring us happiness, we become dependent on things outside our control, which is not ideal to a stoic. This doesn't mean we live an inactive life, but this means that our sense of joy should come from how we think and act within ourselves.

There is nothing wrong with trying to achieve wealth and power, but to the stoic, if it works out you should be happy, but you shouldn't depend on achieving that success to be happy. Otherwise your happiness will be inconsistent, taken away, or never achieved. Stoicism suggests that a successful person is someone who can be okay without the things he or she typically desires for comfort.

This doesn't mean stoics are people without emotion, though. They see human emotion as something that can be trumped by reason, because the position we take towards that emotion decides our mood. There's a quote from Marcus Aurelius that sums it up nicely - "Almost nothing material is needed for a happy life for he who has understood existence."

A stoic's ability to find happiness despite what occurs around them is developed through character and perspective. Nothing is good or bad inherently. Only our judgement and interpretations can be good or bad. A stoic strives for acceptance and indifference towards the events around them and focuses their attention on controlling their reactions.

The practice of stoicism is not easy, and it's impossible to be a perfect stoic that has no negative reactions or desires. However, stoicism gives us a target to strive for. As such, a common stoic practice is to stop oneself from indulging in the things that give them pleasure and comfort to prove to themselves how strong they are.

This practice is to prepare a stoic for situations where they will face physical hardships and to help train the stoic to not desire things outside their control. You can think of this like a dopamine fast but with a different ruleset. A dopamine fast is meant to starve you of anything that provides dopamine for 24 hours to reset and refresh your mind, but for the stoic practice, it is more lenient because it is meant to build character. As for the stoic exercise to deal with negativity, it is called negative visualization.

You simply imagine bad things that will happen to you. Marcus Aurelius used this daily when he had to confront people who weren't so nice to deal with. By starting the day with negative visualization, he was able to be mentally prepared to confront those people. You might think that negative visualization will make your day worse, but it can make your day better when you realize all these bad things you visualized didn't happen to you. Another exercise is memento mori, which is the stoic reminding themselves that life is temporary and short. This way, he or she won't waste time on trivial things.

Life is short, and that is why it is important to direct our energy towards the important things. Stoicism can help give us guidance in this chaotic world full of distractions by helping us find peace from within.

Stoicism Rules to Follow in the Modern Era

1. **Become Honest** - This can take you so far in your journey to become a successful modern stoic. Just be honest in whatever you do and whatever you

say. Being honest can save a lot of your time and the time of others, too. Whether in a relationship, professional commitment, or any other connection, honesty is at the core of being a stoic in the modern day.

2. **Stay comfortable** - Some modern people are used to this already, but I have to emphasize this trait for everyone. Your dressing, living, and general behavior has to be in a flow of comfort. This is a way to remain in harmony with yourself and your life, allowing stoicism to come more easily.

3. **Make your way** - If the path is not obvious, make your way. This mindset can save you from facing failures and backlashes. Just by changing your attitude about how you see things can be the biggest step of your life. Time has changed, so you too have to change yourself.

4. **Be real** - In both your expectations and your promises, be realistic. Your real intentions and words can save your heart from getting broken. Being real is the biggest key to modern stoicism and it can also be taught to children. They learn how to behave and what they can expect from others.

5. **Cut out ego from your life** - Ego can be your biggest enemy. You have to phase it out of your behavior to become contented and successful. An egoistic person can lose everything they care about. Thus, modern stoicism is all about being realistic and free from any negativity.

Stoicism can be applied to modern life quite effectively. But, there can also be some limitations to the stoic philosophy. For example, a stoic has to give up on some important things. By giving up on something, you may realize that your priorities will suffer. You may act oddly to your family and close friends.

When someone faces his or her fears, insecurities, and gives an analyzing shift to their thoughts, it can become difficult. As stoicism is not an easy practice, you may find it hard to cut down on your desires and to live a life on strict values.

The implementation period of stoicism can be really long. It may be difficult to change or adapt to new behaviors and habits. The amount of time it takes can vary from person to person, since we can't change ourselves in just a matter of a few days. You may also feel the urge to deviate back to your non-stoic life, but it is worth a try to become a stoic.

Being stoic is a cumbersome process. You may find it hard to stay committed to doing the meditations. But, make sure you are willing to read some books like this one and see if you can get your friends and family members to discuss stoicism with you.

If you find it difficult to adapt the methods and teachings of stoicism, find a mentor. Someone who has already applied these methods in their own life. Or, if you want to keep it private, read books and study the philosophy to add to your stoic knowledge.

.   .   .

Controlling emotions might be troublesome for you in some situations. The fact that it is troublesome may also bother you. You may find it a little draining psychologically while practicing stoic behavior. Don't lose hope. You can always mix and match the old and modern stoicism and see what works for you and what does not.

8

REAPING THE BENEFITS OF STOICISM

After just a general overview of this book I think you might agree that the fundamental benefits of stoicism are rather clear. All the same, we live in a complex world in which many nuances need to be taken into consideration. In this chapter we will take a closer look at just how the benefits of Stoicism might manifest in one's life.

Greater Accountability for Our Actions

Without a doubt, one of the most powerful benefits of stoicism is its ability for people to take accountability for their actions. And in today's world of incessant blame and victimhood mentality—Stoicism serves to strip away this false veneer and show people that at the end of the day, they are indeed responsible for their actions.

If you do something wrong you can't blame your parents, you can't blame society, and you can't blame your personal circumstances. Stoicism after all is well aware of hardships in life and external forces beyond our control But the Stoic would argue that the one thing that we can control, is our own actions. So, in the mind of the Stoic, anything we do; we are indeed accountable for.

Stoicism helps to bring people out of the self-absorption they are trapped in and teaches them that rather than looking outward for their problems, they need to look inward. Many today, try to negate responsibility for the things they do by blaming others for their behavior. To be sure, there are those who face some real hardship and adversity in life. But for a Stoic it doesn't matter.

Because from the Stoic's perspective adversity is just another word for opportunity. And no matter how many curve balls life may throw you, there is always a way to make the most of it. Yes, you may have been born on the rough side of town, grew up poor and were generally more disadvantaged than most.

But instead of dwelling on these external factors that are out of your control, make the best of the situation and take responsibility for the one thing that is always in your possession—your own actions. Successful people the world over have benefited from this philosophy whether they called themselves a Stoic or not.

Stoicism Helps Shield us from Addiction and Unnecessary Attachment

We all have what the Stoics term "insatiability of desires" if we give in to our impulses. According to Stoicism, desire only leads to more desire, and the more things we get the more we want. This is in itself, the very nature of addiction. The more you drink, do drugs, gamble—whatever the case may be— the more of it you are going to continue to want further down the road.

These things don't satisfy, and only increase desire for them, leading to addiction. Okay, so what's the Stoic solution to this problem? Stepping back and detaching ourselves from the source. Stoicism advises that we need to keep ourselves from vainly chasing after fulfillment, be happy with what we have, and do not so vigorously cling to our possessions / desires that we become addicted to them.

Because addiction is not only a disease—it's slavery. Seneca described it as thus, "So in all our plans and activities, let us do just what we are accustomed to do when we approach a sidewalk vendor who is selling some merchandise or other: let's see what it will cost to get this thing we have our hearts set on. The thing for which nothing is paid often comes at the highest price. I can show you many things whose pursuit and acquisition has cost us our freedom. We would belong to ourselves if these things did not belong to us."

Here Seneca makes it clear, being addicted to anything takes away our freedom and enslaves us to whatever it is that we are addicted to. Stoicism helps us to avoid the extremes of such external attachment. Everything in moderation is the goal, and Stoicism forges a clear path toward that end.

Stoic Principles Foster Strong Leadership

The philosophy of Stoicism encourages us to take responsibility for our actions and as such, puts us on the path to be the leader of our own destiny. Good leaders are those that are selfless rather than selfish after all, and Stoicism specializes in helping us to take the focus off of ourselves and our own misguided perceptions, and back where it needs to be—on the world and how we can do our part to make it a better place.

While a Stoic acknowledges there are outside forces at work, outside of their control, the Stoic knows that they can by their own effort make the situation as good as it can be. This is why Stoicism is naturally conducive for leadership. Here's an interesting example of that in play—think back to the 1970s when NASA was in the midst of the Apollo space program.

There was an ill-fated mission during this period known as Apollo 13. American astronauts were on their way to the moon when damaged equipment nearly cost all of them their lives. The mission leader was a guy named Jim Lovell. If any astronaut was ever a Stoic, Mr. Lovell certainly was.

Because when he realized that one of the onboard oxygen tanks vital to the mission—vital to their very lives—had blown, he stayed completely calm and in the moment. Even though there was a good chance that he and all his crew would soon die, with their craft a veritable coffin forever listlessly drifting in space—did he panic?

No, he did not. Lovell knew full well the situation they were in, yet he calmly—most would say Stoically—radioed ground control to state the famous words, "Houston we have a problem." He didn't shout, "Oh my God! Houston—we're going to die! What are you going to do?"

Despite the massive external threat that loomed, Lovell merely stated the facts as he saw them, and nothing more. Lovel kept a cool, calm, analytical head, and thanks to his rational disposition he was able to formulate a plan with Mission Control that would enable the Apollo team to cut their losses and come home.

The ingenuity of Lovel and his fellow astronauts has since been widely hailed as one of NASA's greatest success stories. This is a prime example of how a strong leader at the helm can take what was initially an abject failure and turn it into a triumph. This of course is just one example, but it demonstrates perfectly well, how Stoic principles do indeed foster strong leadership.

Reduce Stress with a Stoic Lifestyle

For anyone dealing with a lot of stress, Stoic philosophy is tailor made to relieve it! Stoics realized that much of the stress and anxiety that we experience is due to things that are out of our control. We worry about the past and the future for example, but have no control over either one. Yesterday is gone and we have no control over what the future might hold.

Stoics however, teach how one can take things one day at a time and focus on the present instead of worrying about what's outside of their reach. And this holds true for every externality we may face. Stoicism allows us to let go of our anxiety and instead focus on what is in our power to change in the moment. For those who find themselves becoming overwhelmed by all the what if's in life—this is absolutely crucial for reliving stress.

It's also good to keep a journal. Keeping a journal of your daily life may seem a bit trivial at first glance, but Stoics of all stripes have greatly valued the meditation that can be placed upon routine journal entries. In fact, this was the sole express purpose of Marcus Aurelius' "Meditations." It was his personal journal.

As much as others have benefited from his wise entries, he primarily kept the journal to help himself. He never intended to publish his entries. It was simply a way for him to relieve stress at the time. By journaling his thoughts and feelings, he was able to release any pent-up anxiety he may have felt. And if it was good enough for him, this aspect of the Stoic lifestyle will most certainly be good for you too.

Stoicism Makes us Happy

The impetus that kickstarted many philosophies in the first place, has always been the search for happiness—Stoicism among them. Stoics are especially focused on finding happiness. How? By being happy with what they have. Stoicism tells us that the reason why people are dissatisfied is because they are always looking for fulfillment outside of themselves and then become disappointed when they cannot find it.

The problem with basing your happiness on external factors is just that—*they are external.* This is why Stoicism lets us know that the best way to find happiness is to find it from within. The Stoic therefore is primed to only invest their happiness in things that are well within their control.

For the happiness that a Stoic is directed to find is not one that is fleeting but one that will last. This Stoic happiness, that they call, "eudaimonia" which roughly translates as "the good life." The Stoic take on the good life is not one of excess, but of quite literally living a good, and virtuous life.

Stoics believed that happiness resulted as a natural consequence of being good. When you are helpful to others for example, it just might make you feel good and put a smile on your face. If you talk to anyone who regularly volunteers their time in service for others, they will tell you the most rewarding thing about it is the happiness that they feel from serving a greater good.

Stoic Virtue Prevents Snap Judgment

We live in a judgmental world and many of us are used to making snap judgments at a moment's notice. In some regard, this is only natural. As a part of human development along the way, we have learned to jump to quick conclusions out of a necessity for our survival in a dangerous and uncertain world.

If for example, you were walking down a dark alley and see a large hulking figure walking toward you with a knife. In this circumstance most would forgive you for tensing up, and making a snap judgment that your life might be in danger. But other than in extreme situations, the judgments we make are often far from accurate.

And in the world of social media in which every aspect of our lives is often on display, the propensity for glaring misjudgment is so profound, it is appalling. Stoicism helps us to slow down and consider the situation very carefully before we start judging. This can be useful in a wide variety of situations and settings in life.

It's an active process however, so if you find yourself tempted to make a snap judgement against someone or something, pause your thought processes for a moment and remind yourself that you don't might not know all the facts. If you can actively disrupt judgmental thoughts as soon as they occur, you will soon cease to have them altogether.

This Stoic method has actually been so effective that it's been picked up and used in what we now call "Cognitive Behavioral Therapy" (CBT). As we will discuss later in this book, this so-called modern therapy is really only different from Stoicism in name. Because CBT, just like Stoicism, asks you to step back from your preconceived notions and see the world as it really is.

It's Good for Our Physical and Mental Well Being

We live in a world of high anxiety, and it's easy to get over-whelmed. Stoicism however, allows us to step back from what we are doing and take a deep breath.

Stoics knew that the true source of anxiety was in worrying over things that they could not control. People worried about what others thought, they worried about what might happen in the future, and a whole host of other things that were beyond their direct control.

The Stoics therefore taught that it was necessary to let go of these things we could not change and instead take liberty in the things that we could. It is a very freeing experience. Stoics also value moderation in food, drink, and all other things that could be done in excess. This in turn leads to a healthier physical lifestyle. As it turns out, a little bit of Stoicism, just like moderation, is good for both body and mind.

Stoicism Eases the Fear of Death

Stoicism tackles perhaps the greatest fear of all in its efforts to unmask death. Stoics teach us that death is nothing to fear, it is simply a natural process. Stoics realized that the reason why people feared death so much, was because it presented itself as a complete unknown. But Stoicism allows one to rationalize what death really is and thereby take the sting right out of it.

· · ·

As of the writing of this book, much of the world is in the grip of the pandemic outbreak known as the Coronavirus.

History will record how much various populaces panicked during this epidemic, and how many looked at the threat with a calm resolve.

We will remember how many cast a suspicious eye toward their neighbor and how many extended a hand to help. Stoicism does not encourage anyone to be needlessly reckless, but it also firmly advocates courage, even in the face of death.

The Stoic Mindset Gives Us Good Perspective

One of the best benefits about the Stoic mindset is that it gives us good perspective on life. Sometimes we can become so self-absorbed that we feel the whole world revolves around us. Stoicism however, serves to remind one of how insignificant they really are! The idea might sound like a negative one at first, but upon closer examination its actually quite freeing.

Just think about it. Half the time we think things are important, when they are really not important at all. And other times we fret and worry about stuff that we have no business worrying about in the first place. There are all kinds of trivial circumstance that we can obsess over, but in the grand scheme of things many of them really don't matter at all.

.   .   .

Let's say it's announced that you're getting a new supervisor on your job. You don't know anything about this person, yet you spend the whole week worrying about what kind of person they are, if they are going to drastically change work protocol, and whether or not they are going to like you. This is completely useless.

You can't control who the company hires, and even if there are some changes in store, the best you can do is roll with the punches.

And that goes for any situation in life, there's no guarantee that there might not be hardship in the short term, but the level of importance we place on situations is usually far greater than we merit. And as soon as we realize it's not nearly as big of a deal as we make it—we can breathe a huge sigh of relief as a result. The Stoic mindset helps to keep these things in perspective.

Stoicism Gets us Better in Tune with Our Emotions

If someone hears the word Stoic, they usually think of someone or something that is devoid of emotion. But on the contrary, stoicism actually helps to get better in tune with your emotions. It was not the goal of the Stoics to get rid of emotion, they just wanted to get rid of irrational inflamed passion that led to distress and discord.

.   .   .

This is because Stoicism helps us to realize when an emotional reaction is valid and when it is not. When we have an emotional reaction, it is because we are agreeing to be provoked by something. Whether that reaction be a pleasant or an unpleasant one, we are the ones allowing it to transpire. The Stoics sought to prevent such inflamed passion from overriding their sense of reason.

Often enough people act and do things in the moment that are not only contrary to their best interests but contrary to their own emotions. Just imagine the quarreling couple who love each other dealing. The real emotion they feel for each other is love and affection. But trivial arguments have led them to give in to darker impulses of anger and rage, belying the true emotional attachment that they feel for each other.

This is why even a loved one if driven into passionate excess enough, could slam a door in your face and scream that they "hate you" when in reality this is far from the case. This example is maybe a little extreme, but we see similar things all the time. We speak of how people sometimes say things they don't really mean because they were "caught up in the moment." But this is exactly what the Stoics seek to avoid. They do not want to be caught up in the brief moment of inflamed passion, and thereby negate the true intentions of their heart. It is in this fashion that the Stoics enabled themselves to stay focused on what really mattered to them, and get in rightful tune with their emotions as a result.

It is for this reason that it is important once again to press the pause button when you feel that you are on the verge of being overwhelmed by emotion. Many of us can feel that upswell of emotional angst as it happens, and if you train ourselves well enough, we can disrupt it and replace it with rational thought. Stoicism helps us to do just that.

Stoicism Helps to Foster Greater Acceptance

Domineering people who seek to curb the actions and opinions of others, are some of the most unhappy and unfulfilled individuals you could ever meet. Because no matter how tyrannical one's disposition, there will always be external forces that remain firmly outside of their personal jurisdiction.

By contrast, the more one accepts this fact, the more accepting they are of other people as a consequence. The Stoic could be in the room with any given number of people with any given number of opinions and beliefs, and get along with all of them just fine. Just because someone doesn't agree with you, doesn't mean you need to argue with them, or shut them out.

The Stoic intuitively knows to value the differences among people even if it's not something that they themselves personally buy into. A Stoic could be a lone conservative in the midst of a bunch of liberals for example, and it wouldn't matter in the least. For a Stoic, a mere difference in opinion would not render any verdict on how they value an individual.

. . .

In the toxic political environment of today, it would do all of us some good to take on the example of such Stoic tolerance. Political polarization would be a thing of the past if we would simply learn to respect differences in opinion. And if you apply the principles of stoicism to your life, it will indeed foster greater acceptance of others as a result. And you will find yourself all the happier for it.

9
———

HOW TO PRACTICE STOICISM IN DIFFERENT CONTEXTS

Stoicism in Your Workplace

We all know that the modern workplace can be a minefield. Every time that you bring people from diverse backgrounds and of different characters together in one space, there is bound to be some degree of conflict and egotism. Therefore, the office is the perfect place to apply Stoic principles.

No matter what kind of work you are engaged in, the Stoic philosophy can help you achieve clarity and peace of mind.

Avoid the tendency to make things more difficult than they should be

Workplace relationships can be tricky. There are some coworkers or bosses that are simply a pain to work with and they can make the workplace very frustrating. Let's say that one of these frustrating coworkers requests something from you. Your immediate reaction is to refuse, not because you can't do the job, but because you simply don't get along with them. You come up with some inane excuses and they, in turn, get angry and start yelling. Before you know it, they too refuse to honor an earlier request you had made and the conflict gets worse.

Don't allow external objects influence your mind

There are days when work can feel extremely laborious or your boss may be too demanding. You start walking around the office lamenting about how overwhelmed you feel and how frustrating your manager is. But from a Stoic point of view, this is simply not possible. How can external objects overwhelm or frustrate you yet your inner Self is supposed to be in control?

Focus on the task at hand

The solution is to fix your mind only on what is in front of you. Do your job as if it was the last task you will ever do, and like a good Roman soldier, stop complaining and engaging in irrational sideshows. Set yourself apart from all the people who want to waste time gossiping at the water cooler and simply find clarity in mastering your craft.

Stop working out of habit

As a Stoic, you should not allow yourself to be a slave to your habits. Routine behavior can quickly lull you into a sense of comfort, and this is not always the best thing at the workplace. If you are not the kind of employee who thinks on their feet and comes up with innovative solutions, your head may be first on the chopping block. Train yourself to always ask: Are the methods I'm using really the best way to solve this?

Value your freedom and peace of mind

You have to constantly reevaluate your life, especially with regard to your job. Millions of people have sold their souls for a paycheck, convincing themselves that this is all life has to offer. We have accepted dysfunctional jobs that are making us sick, keeping us away from our families, and stealing our peace of mind. So you have to ask yourself: Is your current workplace environment right for you?

Don't let your job be your only trophy

A Stoic takes pride in their life mission, but they do not get too attached that they somehow lose sight of the bigger picture. You may love your job a lot, but it should never be a life sentence. There are many people who lose their jobs abruptly and simply go crazy. They either commit suicide or grab a gun and attack their ex-employer.

Friendship and Love in a Stoic Life

People who fall in love at first sight will often let their emotions get the best of them. They sometimes even use this as an excuse for the way they behave or the way that they treat others. But this is completely against the beliefs that most Stoics have and can be a dangerous way to live your life.

Stoics take a slightly different method of finding love and being with someone. They may have times when they fall madly in love with someone they just met. But instead of just jumping right in and following their own emotions, they choose to take a different course instead. When they meet this person, they stop and think it through, and they take things slowly. Rather than just jumping in and moving in with the other person right away, they will take their time to get to know the other person.

The idea of love for a Stoic is one that is moderated by a sense of loss in the future, by the potential for betrayal, from the chance that our feelings towards that person could also change over time. After accepting these conditions, the irrational of these powerful feelings of love become a bit more rational, and the life of a Stoic is more manageable.

As someone who loves virtue, the Stoic is able to recognize when others have virtue as well. And since this kind of disposition is the foundation for the happiness of a Stoic, unrequited love is just seen as absurd to the Stoic. Due to the active disposition, the Stoic lover is going to spend their time worrying more about giving love to other people, rather than receiving it. They do enjoy receiving love from other people, but they follow the idea that it is better to give than to receive when it comes to love. Once they find someone worthy of their love, and they know that this love will allow them to still pursue what is important to them and allow them to think rationally, then the Stoic is more than happy to share their love with that person.

Thus, life having your friends around is most helpful because one never endures those torments or aggravations linked with driving a lonely and friendless life. Fulfilling desire is excellent since it frees oneself from the oppression of that longing and desire.

The stoic love is directed by a feeling of future misfortune, through the possibility for disloyalty, for the truth that one's very own sentiments or feelings may change after some time also. Having acknowledged these essential conditions, the irrationality of these great biological feelings, a person has become a bit more rational and life somewhat more manageable.

The Stoics as a lover of virtues, perceive virtue or uprightness in others. Furthermore, since individuals, virtuous disposition and not really to obtain sex or love-is the establishment for their joy, or unrequited love is ludicrousness from Stoic standpoints. Because of this dynamic disposition, the Stoic lovers are likely to prioritize giving love more than getting it. Receptive to this entire thing-the world, the universe, and humanity and at certain extent loved by it, a lover can give up the love for a particular person. Individualized love isn't irrelevant, a long way from it, yet it isn't the essence and extent of affection and love.

· · ·

The Stoic love is governed by the idea of a future loss or even a potential betrayal or even the reality that our very own feelings for a person may change over time. To accept these basic conditions makes life a little more manageable when the inevitable does happen. The Stoics, being a lover of virtue, recognizes the virtue in other people.

The Stoic lover will prioritize giving love over receiving it. The Stoic lover can relinquish this love of the specific. Individualized love is important, but it is not the be all and end all for the essence of love. Taking this idea, the Stoic approaches love like a General in the army, equipped with a cool head and a strategic plan. He or she carries out the antidotes of Romantic excess; they are ready to love but will not fall in love. If they do fall in love, as we all humans are inclined to do, they are a way of how to pick themselves up again. As a Stoic, you are welcome to love. Love your friends. Love your spouse or the one you are with. Love your children. Most of all, love anyone else who is important in your life— and when you love them, make sure to do it deliberately and deeply. The Stoic philosophy is not against love and everything that comes with it. Instead of just jumping into this and making rash decisions without reason, take a clear-headed approach. Instead of falling in love, choose to be in love with the other person. This can lead to a deeper connection than you can imagine, allows both you and the other person to keep your own unique personalities without giving anything up, and can lead to a deeper love with that person.

Stoicism in Business

Is it possible to use Stoic philosophy and principles to build a successful business? In this section, you will learn how to put into practice your Stoic beliefs as an entrepreneur.

Stoicism is perfect for any entrepreneur who wants to learn how to deal with the ups and downs of running a company. Here are Stoic strategies that will enable you to run your company with effectiveness, clarity, and peace of mind.

Associate with the Right People

If you want to grow your business and succeed, you have to associate with other like-minded entrepreneurs. Don't just let anyone join your inner sanctum. This doesn't mean that you should become a snob and ignore certain groups of people. But as an entrepreneur who wants to achieve certain goals, you want to be around people who inspire you to become better. Better yet, your associates should be entrepreneurs who have already been where you want to go.

Prepare for Business Failure

This is where you have to use the Stoic technique of negative visualization. When you come up with plans for your business, always try to visualize the negative things that may occur to thwart you. This prepares you for any eventuality and prevents disappointment from crippling you.

· · ·

Some people call this pessimism but it's always best to be prepared. Come up with alternative plans that will bail you out in case things don't work out.

Invest in Yourself

Everyone wants to start their own business these days. People see entrepreneurship as the fastest way to get rich. While this may be true to an extent, you also need to realize that there are many risks and challenges you will have to contend with. There are long working hours, many stressful days, and countless sleepless nights. As an entrepreneur, never forget that the greatest company you can ever build is you. Go ahead and invest your capital in whatever startup you want, but don't forget to invest in becoming a better human being every day.

Don't Follow the News

The kind of news that is available today can be very manipulative and incorrect. If you are depending on the news to make business decisions, you may not last very long in the market. There is a lot of fake news and irrelevant information on social media that will not help you grow and build your business in the long term. You need to resist that urge to waste time checking your Twitter or Facebook feed every five minutes.

Focus on Things You Can Control

. . .

As an entrepreneur, you can go ahead and set goals, but make sure that those goals are internal. A good example is pitching an investor when you need some financing. Instead of setting the goal of convincing the investor to give you their money, your goal should be to present the best possible pitch you can. This takes the pressure off and you then focus on what you can control. If the investor chooses not to invest, then there's no need to be unhappy. You gave it your best.

Strive for Value, not Wealth

You can go much further and provide value to your fellow humans. Make your business valuable to the local community by offering things that people value. That should be your duty. See your customers as your boss and make their lives better.

Control Your Emotions

Circumstances are not responsible for how we feel. It is our perceptions that dictate our emotions. As a Stoic, you need to use logic and reason to control any negative emotions. Entrepreneurship can be extremely stressful, especially when you are just starting. There will be rejections, failures, and roadblocks. The best way to avoid suffering from needless stress and anxiety is to change the way you react to situations.

To be stoical in business is to be aware, in control as well as be mindful of what we do, who we engage with, the trends in our industry, expenditure and the day-to-day running of our business entities. We train our minds to be this way rather than get lost in the various emotions and random thought processes that lead us to lose focus on our business goals.

Practicing stoic principles into our business and entrepreneurship as well as in our leadership can help us build resilience and change our state of mind to rebound from knock downs.

Another Stoic principle is to turn problems into opportunity. If you want to cultivate a culture of creativity in your business, then you need to think of 'The Glass half Full, instead of half empty' and to turn obstacles upside down. Look for an opportunity in every bad situation.

Stoicism in School

In school, children learn how to deal with difficult emotions such as worry, frustration, cravings, fear, arguments, temper, gossip, squabbles, jealousy, bitterness, hurt and many other complex emotions. Through stoicism, we can offer more fortifying ways to think about dealing with these difficulties:

Introducing Stoicism to your Students

On their first week of school, you can teach them the approach to life and that everyone experiences difficulties, but we all have it in us to overcome these difficulties. You can do this in assemblies or an hour of lesson. You can also discuss this over group. With stoicism, you teach your students to anticipate the frustrations of life as well as the mantra 'Stay Stoical.'

Oftentimes, students will feel upset or even resent your giving them detention. In your conversations with them, remind them to stay stoical, calm as well as help them build and keep a perspective of their detention. Teach them to let go of anger, work out the elements that they can control as well as think about how they can build trust in the future. You can also allow them to decide what they want to do differently next time.

For students, educators can help them see that preparing, revising and overcoming their procrastination is something that is within their control. If they do fail an exam or perform poorly, remember to tell them to remain stoical and not to allow this minor complication agitate them. Instead, tell them to focus on what they can do differently the next time around and help them with their upcoming assessments.

When a student gets into an argument with their fellow students or friends, using stoicism here can help to remind both parties to practice calm, ignore vicious rumors as well as ignore gossip and insults. It also helps them to stay positive or rational rather than give in to these negative thoughts and exacerbate anger and mistrust.

It is definitely a struggle to wake up early and get to school and it is even harder if students are feeling ill. Of course, if they are feeling well but lack the motivation to get up and come to school, use stoicism to help them see that waking up anyway, showing up anyway is something to be proud of. Help students see that some setbacks can be controlled. If they fall, get back up and try again. If they colored outside the lines, then create your own masterpiece. The idea here is that a stoic mindset reduces our fragility. The volatility of the world itself cannot destabilize us. With the use of stoicism, problems can become opportunities as long as we train our resilience.

Sports are competitive by nature and at times, tempers can run high. The use of stoicism here can help students not to over-celebrate their wins and jeer those who did not win a match or score a goal. On the other hand, not winning also teaches us not to despair or put on the blame game. Using stoicism prevents a footballer from turning a yellow card into a red card or from getting a contestant from being disqualified. If there are any setbacks, great-here's a chance to train our willpower.

Growing up, children also face difficult times. As much as we would like to shelter them from the adversities of life, children also face issues and problems of their own with their friends, peers, siblings, and cousins. If they are taught to remain stoical in school, then they can cascade these learnings to their own family life by enabling them to deal with arguments and adversity in their families such as death or divorce. It gives them a good perspective and enables them to remain grateful and not take the people around them for granted. Rather, they develop meaningful relationships with their immediate family members, which then transcends into their adult lives.

. . .

Teaching children to remain stoic during tough times creates a powerful perspective for them that helps them to improve their resilience, their relationships and also their lives.

Stoic Advice for Parenting

Most parents would never even think that Stoicism would have anything to offer them in terms of parenting advice. However, you will be surprised just how encompassing Stoic principles are when it comes to running a home and raising children.

Of course, raising a kid in today's society is nothing like what the Stoics had to deal with in their time. But they did share some great gems that may help the modern parent cope better with their children.

Parents usually wear many hats when it comes to how they raise their children. Most parents often see themselves as playing the role of provider in the family. You go to work, earn some money, stock the fridge, and buy your kids some clothes/toys, and so on. However, there is a critical aspect of parenting that many overlook, and that is the role of teacher.

Stoicism doesn't say that you should not provide for your children. However, you also need to go further and teach them to be responsible, caring, generous, and self-controlled.

Teach your kids to pursue the best in themselves and others so that they will end up living a virtuous life.

Kids may be cute and cuddly but there are times when they are a menace and act stupid. This can leave any parent feeling angry and terribly frustrated. However, Seneca had something to say to parents who felt like losing their temper over their kids.

When you feel overwhelmed by kids who are acting like fools and refusing to listen to you, try not to focus on all the negative things in your life. You are alive and have a family, which is more than most people can claim. Yes, they are acting badly right now, but you know you love them and they love you too. Life can be much worse than that, can't it? Always be grateful.

By teaching your children to reflect on their actions and contemplate their future, you are raising them to be responsible. They will realize that making mistakes is normal as long as you own up, learn your lesson, and not repeat them.

Punishing Your Kids

It is inevitable that one of your kids will do something wrong that deserves some kind of punishment. But does that mean you should immediately do so when you are still angry?

.   .   .

The Stoic way to handle this would be to give your child the chance to speak up in his defense. Listening to what they have to say is a good way to give yourself the time to get rid of your anger. Your raw emotions will dissipate and you will then make sure that your punishment matches the mistake the child made.

Punishing children is a sensitive issue. You want to prevent them from repeating the mistake but at the same time, you want them to understand why they deserve punishment. Take the time to hear your child out and pick a fair way to reprimand them.

If a child demands something in anger, do not give it to them. Wait until they have calmed down and then offer them what they had asked for. If you are a wealthy parent, let your kids see the wealth but don't allow them to use it. If they make a mistake, correct them. Finally, don't spend too much money on your kids because they will begin to see themselves as being better than others due to the lavish lifestyle they are accustomed to.

Stoicism for Financial Success

Some of the early Stoics were quite wealthy and powerful. So what lessons can we learn from these men about how to use the Stoic philosophy to create financial success? You will learn five key Stoic strategies that will help you achieve financial success.

Your Salary Doesn't Matter

. . .

In other words, you can get wealthy by reducing your appetite for the unnecessary luxuries of life. Most people don't have the habit of saving a portion of their salary. They think that they aren't earning enough to save anything.

Don't Let the Economy/markets Dictate Your Emotions

In the Stoic philosophy, there is neither bad nor good. Everything that happens is dependent on how you react. If your emotions are a product of your inner Self, then that means you can control them. Don't go running around stressing out and making silly financial decisions based on your emotions. You are likely to lose money this way. Stay focused and controlled.

Let the Goal Take Care of Itself

The strategy here is to take your eyes off the goal and concentrate on establishing processes that will help you achieve it. Part of that process is changing the way you think and act toward money. All you have to do is gradually follow your plan day by day and let the big goal take care of itself.

Create and Stick to a Financial Plan

In financial terms, if you set out to achieve wealth without deciding upfront what financial success looks like, you cannot plan for it. You need to stop thinking that creating wealth is something that you can stumble into.

Find a Financial Mentor

If you want to achieve financial success, you need to learn from those who have already done so. Look for a role model who has the qualities that you want to emulate and do what they do. Your financial role model can be someone you interact with in person or it can be someone whom you've never even met.

Those who think Stoicism is limited to keeping a handle on your emotions are wrong. These five financial strategies are based on Stoic principles. Start using them today and you will be well on your way to improving your financial future.

Stoicism in Military Leadership

Stoicism is a way of life that can be applied at any time where leadership is required, not just during difficult times. In the military, a leader must be stoic and never allow their emotions to cloud their judgment. It doesn't matter whether a leader agrees with certain orders or not. As long as the command that is given is legal and moral, you must obey.

Leading a group of soldiers is not easy. You need to be prepared and resilient. By practicing Stoic leadership, you are also ensuring that those who are under your command will also provide good leadership.

. . .

Most people perceive Stoicism as a philosophy that is against any display of emotions at all. However, Stoicism is primarily concerned with distinguishing the things that you can control and those you can't. For a Stoic, the only things that you should value most are those that are within your control.

Stoicism is built on discipline, and without maintaining discipline, there will be no link between the leaders and followers. A good leader needs to be disciplined enough to lead a team, while the team also needs to be disciplined enough to take orders from the leader.

When a military officer fails to act in a professional manner, it's because they were unable to take control of their emotions. Being filled with negative emotions like greed, envy, fear, and anger is a recipe for unprofessionalism.

Leadership is not just for those who sit at the top of the hierarchy. It is virtually impossible for one person to lead a whole unit alone. It will be difficult to communicate to every single junior officer or subordinate about their specific duties. There must be a leader at every level of the chain of command.

Stoic leadership is a way of life that can change the lives of the leader and everyone who works for them. Officers must have the character, strength, and determination to lead with a sense of duty. Military leaders must be able to sacrifice everything for their team, and this kind of moral selflessness is what allows one to overcome the fear of death itself.

10

IMPLEMENTING STOICISM IN YOUR DAILY LIFE

L et's get on to stoic exercises that you can start applying today.

Stoic Exercises to Change Your Life

Negative Visualization

Optimism is a dark side when you reflect a belief or hope that your life or a specific aspect of it is going to be favorable and positive. You possibly set yourself up for disappointment. That's why so many people start their day with a positive attitude and get defeated by the harsh and ugly realities of life by the end. Stoics have a way to counter-attack life's ugliness using a technique called negative visualization.

Negative visualization actually takes strength from pessimism by mentally preparing you for undesirable and uncomfortable situations. Marcus Aurelius said the following regarding this: "Begin each day by telling yourself 'Today I shall be meeting with interference, ingratitude, insolence, disloyalty, ill-will, and selfishness.'" By visualizing the negativity combined with an accepting attitude, Marcus Aurelius managed his expectations and shielded his soul against adversity to achieve self-control.

Practicing the ability to control oneself can be very useful in order to stay away from addictive behavior and acting on your impulses when it's better not to, and to remain focused on the things that truly matter to you. Stoics make a clear distinction between the things we can control and the things we cannot control. Epictetus said that things which are in our control are: our opinions, pursuit, desire, and aversion. This directly points towards our actions. Things which are not in our control can be explained as whatever we can't control by our own actions. The key is strengthening the things in our control, which takes practice.

There are different ways to do this. An example is intermittent fasting, in which you don't eat for a specific amount of time. Another example is chewing your food a certain number of times before you swallow it. The last one seems easy, but when you're a glutton like me, when it comes to food it's actually very difficult.

The last method is to practice not giving up. After swallowing your food, or after chewing it for ten to twenty times, why don't you start eating like a pig? Don't use your hands and just go for it, especially in a restaurant so everyone can see what you're doing. This is a way to combat a trait that most of us have—caring too much about the opinions of other people.

The thing is, the opinions of other people are not up to

you, so why worry about them? Because of our social conditioning, it takes practice to break this habit. A fear of social ostracism is deeply ingrained within us. By deliberately making a fool of ourselves, we will be exposed to situations in which people will judge us negatively even if it's just through looks or giggles. Slowly, you'll experience that this doesn't hurt as you've imagined. Thus, you don't give up and your attitude will become stronger.

Journaling

Journaling entails writing down your thoughts and is a practice used by Stoics to find relief and create order in their thoughts and memories. As a result, journaling has a highly cathartic effect on the mind. Marcus Aurelius is perhaps the most famous Stoic who kept a journal. In fact, his journal is available in book form and has been mentioned or quoted numerous times. This work was never intended to be published because it was Marcus' personal diary. Epictetus and Seneca, both Stoic philosophers, kept journals in some form. Seneca spoke about it in the following words: "When the light has been removed and my wife has fallen silent, aware of this habit that's now mine, I examine my entire day and go back over what I've done and said, hiding nothing from myself, passing nothing by."

Memento Mori

"Remember you must die." The practice of memento mori means reminding ourselves that we are going to die.

Thinking about the reality of death puts your life in perspective and tells you that your life is ticking away second by second, and that we should not waste it on trivial things. Also, it teaches us to live life more fully because tomorrow we might as well be dead. Thinking about death should not evoke fear, but gratitude and appreciation for the life that has been given to us. Seneca said that we should be prepared for death. He said we should postpone nothing and live our lives to the fullest. Someone who lives as if it is their last day can never run out of life.

View From Above

Think about the fact that the Earth is a simple sphere zooming around in space. This sphere that is our home is just a small planet in our solar system and completely dwarfed by the bigger planets like Jupiter and Saturn, and let's not even take into account the Sun. The Sun itself is a small star compared to many other stars in our solar system, which is just one of the many many systems in the Milky Way. When we realize how small we are, it becomes much easier to let go of the many trivialities of our human existence.

That annoying co-worker, your mother-in-law, the guy who cut you off in traffic—none of these things are significant anymore. When we see them from a cosmic point of view, even larger events like wars, natural disasters, and other tragedies are minor events. If we realize how vast the universe is, we realize how small we are. It's humbling and it puts our existence in perspective. Once we arrive at this new perspective, occasionally it makes us giggle at people who are trig-gered and upset by stupid, meaningless things.

Now for the view from above exercise. Firstly, picture yourself in the same room outside of your body looking upon your-self. Now pay attention to yourself and everyone around you on the same floor of your house. Now picture everyone in your house, with yourself at the center. Now zoom out and picture everyone that's on your street. You'll picture everyone in your neighborhood. Zoom out again with you in the center and imagine everyone in your city, each with their own indi-vidual lives. Now imagine everyone in your country. Zoom all the way out as if you're looking at Google Maps. Imagine everyone's problems, and finally zoom out to where you're looking at Earth. Picture all the people in different countries, each with their own individual lives, each with their own problems, each with their own families. This exercise is a good way to help you overcome emotional hurdles and put things in perspective.

Amor Fati

When we worry, we are concerned about a particular outcome. We want the future to be such and such, and we fear the possibility of things going completely wrong. Worrying about the future causes anxiety, and the Stoics have a simple remedy for this known as Amor Fati. "Amor fati" is a Latin phrase that means "loving fate." Whatever happens in your life, you'll be fine as long as you accept the outcome. This does not imply that we should become cynical and do nothing. Goals and ambitions are fine as long as they are not tied to the outcome. Assume you are a musician. You work as hard as you can and write the best music you can, but you remain unconcerned about the outcome. Simultaneously, your focus will shift from a concept and goal somewhere in the future to the present moment, relieving you of the burden of worrying about unfavorable outcomes. As a result, your work improves and your chances of success increase.

Talk Less

This one might be a little difficult for the professional speaker or talkative person. But this is the best habit one can acquire. Only talk when it is required, and instead listen more attentively. Also endeavor never to speak when you are upset or angry. When your emotions are in charge, your brain is not.

Choose Your Company

It is up to you and your own beliefs as far as how you choose to live your life. However, remember that your company is a reflection of you. Thus, make sure you spend your time with the right people. These people can include anyone, family or friends, as long as they are compatible with your view of the world. You should closely pay attention to whom you spend your time with and evaluate if their emotional intelligence level is a match with your own. If someone you associate with isn't a good person, how do you expect them to make your life better? Life is all about the decisions we make, and those decisions include the company we keep. Stoicism reminds us how important it is to value the right friendships and relationships.

Face Insults with Calmness

If someone insults you, try not to respond in kind. There is no reason to react emotionally, especially since it will not make the situation better. In most cases, an insult from someone says more about them than it does about you. If you respond with the same kind of venom, you will be on the same level as they are. Stoicism is about rising above, so treat insults with a calm detachment. They'll have less of an effect on you, and you won't compromise your own image or integrity.

Don't Speak Too Much About Yourself

Extroverts might find this difficult to practice, but trust me, it is remarkable. Don't overshare or brag about your experiences, possessions, qualities, adventures, etc. Other people are often just not that interested. Or, they'll feel like you're more interested in yourself than in them, and there is no better way to end a conversation. There should always be a give and take. Give a small amount of information, then listen attentively.

Speak Without Judging

·   ·   ·

To adopt this habit, you have to start speaking according to the facts. We generally speak about whatever is on our minds, and often we speak hastily. Hasty speaking means hasty judgement. Imagine how much better the world would be if we didn't judge, though. What if we looked at human affairs in a more matter-of-fact manner. If someone drinks a lot, don't call them a drunk. Simply observe that they like a glass of wine now and again. If a friend is often complaining, don't think of them as a downer. Observe that they speak about the events in their life that cause them pain. Unless they ask for your opinion, refrain from giving one, even in your own head. Are there any habits you have that you wouldn't want someone else judging? It's the same for everyone you encounter.

Life is Short, Make the Best of It

Human life is incredibly brief, especially when you take into consideration the timescale of the universe. We are a blip on the map, and yet we waste the little time we have feeling sad, hurt, angered, and focus on all the wrong things. We become obsessed with wealth, material possessions, and our reputations, none of which will matter once we're gone. Stoicism wants you to remember that. Remember how brief it all is, and add back that sense of wonder to your life. Marvel at the fact that you exist at all. When you realize that you're less than a grain of sand in this wide universe, you appreciate yourself and your life more.

Get Inspiration

. . .

A stoic will often seek someone who can act as a mentor. Set a role model for your life and try to adapt their behavior. A role model can be like your guardian angel who will guide you to a better way of life. This inspiration can be anyone, from a member of your family to a friend.

Discomfort

Don't be afraid to feel some discomfort every now and again. This could be in the form of sleeping on the floor, eating at a cheap restaurant, buying items from a dollar store instead of brand names, etc. Try this once or twice a month to remember how much you should appreciate the simple pleasures and small comforts that you're able to afford or have access to.

Sickness and Pain are Opportunities

Do you feel in pain while you are sick? Are you intolerant to the misery? This exercise can be good for you. Turn your pain into an opportunity and see how tolerant you become. According to stoicism, pain belongs to the body, not the mind. So, you can feel the pain through the body but not through the mind. For example, if you have a fever, take it as an opportunity to rest. In this way, you will no longer see pain as a hindrance.

Opportunity

· · ·

Opportunity abounds in this world, but most of us are blind to it. We fill our minds with junk that blocks out the real experiences and the opportunities, then we complain that we can't move forward in life. I've experienced this, and it's pretty straightforward. Do you think about it the amount of energy you get back when you're not dissipating it all that? Be conscious that your unconscious mind isn't chewing on all that stuff from the nonsense pop culture TV, must watch shows, whatever to the news and the echo-chamber of fear that's created in the world. When you separate yourself at a healthy level and of course you choose to engage, you're a good citizen and a good participant in society. But you draw some bright line boundaries around it. You get so much energy back that's astonishing. And one of the things you may want to care a lot less about is the social comparison side of what other people are doing. Maybe a little less Twitter, a little less Instagram and a little more of what you're here to do would be a good idea.

Epictetus was an old-school, intense teacher. He was a former slave who then became freed and then he became a prominent stoic philosopher. So he had a school where a lot of the young kind of nobility came to training. He was a super intense guy. He was the greatest influence on Marcus Aurelius. What's interesting is that a Roman Emperor philosopher learned from a former Roman slave the philosophy that he practiced unbelievably diligently.

Then we have Seneca, the third stoic, who was the era's greatest playwright. He was a power broker one of the wealthiest people in Rome. Fascinating trio!

· · ·

The three of them used metaphors around fighting, rustling, and boxing. These were their big metaphors, kind of like how we use basketball and football as metaphors for our lives today. Their sport of choice was something called pankration, which literally means all strength. It's kind of a more pure form of UFC, the mixed martial arts of today. Pankration, full strength. Epictetus would counsel his young nobleman and he would say, "Look, what kind of boxer are you if you're in the ring? You get hit in the face and then you just walk out of the ring." He said, "What kind of boxer are you if you aren't going to get hit?" That's the whole point of competing in that type of sport. It's an opportunity to show up with your full strength, and if you walk out of the ring that actually doesn't have any consequence. But if you get hit in life, which is inevitable, the same way you're going to get hit if you're in a boxing ring, and you walk out of life and you give up, then what kind of boxer are you?

He said that, most importantly, what are you training? For the whole point of your training is that if you're a boxer or a wrestler or whatever a human being is able to be, to deal with a really strong opponent is the whole point. You want the best opponent you can get. You want life to challenge you. You set big, aggressive, exciting goals that are challenging yet doable and meaningful. Knowing you're going to have challenges, and knowing it's going to force you to rise to your absolute best. So when you get hit and you're ready to walk out, thinking about it first. These philosophers' notes and the optimal living classes and all the other work is for you to optimize your life. It is all about being able to deal with life's challenges. You have to remember that this is why you train, that's what you want to say. When you face a challenge, rub your hands together and say "What's the tool and the weapon I need to bring to this battle right now?" Remember that this is about being a warrior of the mind, not a librarian. Be a good life boxer. Show up for opportunity and do your best.

Everything You Have is a Borrowed Item from the Future

Yes, you read that right. Everything can be taken from you in a second. The only thing you have that is truly yours is your mind. And even then, one day you will no longer have a body or mind. Everything from your toes to your phone is borrowed and won't be yours one day. Enjoy everything while you have it. It's all here for a limited time only.

Count Your Blessing

You must stay aware of your blessing. Your family, friends, all of these things are your blessings. You shouldn't ask for things you can't have, just focus on what you already have. On the other hand, you should also not get attached to the things you consider as your blessings. The point of blessings is that they're special and precious, and therefore deserve to be treated with love and respect, not possessiveness.

Don't Blame Someone Who Does Something Wrong to You

When someone does anything to you, it's right according to their perception. You shouldn't blame such a person. Instead, have pity or be kind to them, and don't consider taking revenge. Learn to move on.

Become Tranquil

This exercise is to practice calmness even in adverse situations. It will be worth practicing stoicism by including this exercise. If there is a situation which is making you angry, remind yourself that you have to choose tranquility instead. Seneca talks about a Greek word, "amia," which directly translates as tranquility. How we achieve a state of tranquility?

There are two ways - you need to have a sense of clarity, and you need to know who you are, what's important to you, and then you need to have the courage to live in that way. That's actually the essence of it. What can get in the way of this, however, is self-doubt and a lack of confidence or second guessing yourself. You can feel that something is a part of your path, who you are, and what you are meant to be doing, but then you second-guess that sense. When this happens, your tranquility is gone, you become anxious, and you begin comparing yourself to others.

You feel that you are not keeping up with other people around you or that you encounter. Instead of doing this, ignore what other people are doing and stop second guessing yourself. Stay on your path. Of course it will evolve, but have the confidence, the clarity, and the courage to step forward. That's the essence of tranquility. So think about who you are, what your gifts are, and how you are committed to giving them to the world. Commit to that every day. Do the work to find clarity and move forward.

Daily Lifestyle

Epictetus and Marcus Aurelius taught everyone how to live life through a stoic method. Stoicism permeates our culture in ways a lot of us aren't really familiar with. But often, we wonder where to start. Stoicism is the distinction between that which is within our control and that which is outside of our control. So, the whole practice of stoicism ultimately, or one aspect anyway, the central aspect, comes down to distinguishing between the things that are within our control and the things that are outside of our control.

The wise stoic philosopher is always doing the math, thinking *Is this within my control or not?* And guess what? The only things that are within our control are our thoughts, behaviors, and our response to what's happening in the world. So, we can't change our past, we can't predict with 100% certainty the future, and we can't do anything about what's happening right now. What we can do and what we can control is whether or not we choose to step forward with virtue. Whether we choose to do our best every day.

That's the essence of stoicism, and it's reflected in the serenity prayer. You can adapt the serenity prayer in your daily life and take the maximum benefits of stoicism. In this prayer, you have to ask God (or whatever higher power you believe in) to grant you the serenity to accept the things you can not change and courage to change the things that are under your control. This is the shortest but the strongest exercise in stoicism. You can do it anytime you feel worried, in danger, or in any difficult situation. The ancient philosophers weren't cataloging these ideas much. They weren't librarians of the mind like a lot of modern-day academic philosophers are. They were warriors of the mind they were striving to embody these ideas. No idea was more important than this: knowing what's within our control, knowing what is not, and then choosing to respond.

Acquiescence

Ancient stoics had a couple of practices like reserve clause that we already mentioned,, which basically means that before a stoic does anything, they think *Yes, I want to do this. This is my target, and I'll do it unless something else intervenes.* They always know that the outcome is not within their control, and they call that the reserve clause.

The second practice is what they call the art of acquiescence, or acquiesce to reality. They don't fight reality. If a storm arises while they're at sea, or they get hit in the face when they're in the boxing ring, they don't moan about it and think *Why is this happening to me?* They acquiesced to it. They roll with it, and although it was written about and found thousands of years ago, it is still an amazing practice of stoicism.

· · ·

Stoics said not only should you accept what happens to you via acquiescence, you should also love it. You should love your fate, and act as if you wanted that to happen. Basically, act like you scripted this negative thing, so you can rise up to it.

Any time you try to get rid of something in your life, you also get rid of all of your power. So, the art of acquiescence is again remembering rule number one, which is that the only thing you have control over is your response to a situation. So you have to love what it is.

Think about anything in your life that you might be fighting, and think if you can look at the lesson in that. Use it to get a little bit stronger. That's what you have to become. Better and better. Rub your hands together with challenges rather than run out of the ring. Train yourself to say yes and accept whatever life throws your way.

Ignore the Opinions of Others

There are some important sayings which Marcus said about other people's opinions. Why do we care so much about other people's opinions? We are social creatures, and many of us learn from an early age that we need to fit in. We don't want to be labeled as weird or different, so we conform and try to fit in with everyone else. This behavior starts right from childhood. Children often develop a self-image that is reliant on others. Such people live according to the opinions of others, and this impacts their whole life. They seek approval and some sort of validation from others in the form of praise and approval. This validation tends to make us worried about whether this image is correct or not. So, you're constantly asking for validation from friends, family, colleagues and even complete strangers. Sadly, many of us buy things we don't need with money we don't have to influence strangers or someone whom we don't even like.

This can be easily understood by the Looking-Glass Self Concept. According to this concept, firstly we create an image of how others see us, then we create a judgment of that appearance, and then we create our own self-concept through the judgment of others. We then perceive this judgment to be either favorable or unfavorable. It is utterly wrong to perceive ourselves according to another person's point of view or to see ourselves as another person's opinion. You can't control someone else's opinion, so this is a game that can't be won.

I'll say it again: constantly trying to validate yourself according to others is a doomed practice. You're basically handing over your self-worth to someone else. People's opinions oftentimes have nothing to do with you at all. So why give them this power? No one should have that kind of control over you except yourself. In this way, you are becoming their prisoner.

So, with all that said, this is what Marcus stated about the opinions of others: he said that you should not waste your life for the sake of thoughts of others. A person should be willing to take opinions only from their loved ones. Marcus stressed that everyone can be wrong at some point in their life, so don't worry about what others say, let alone their opinions. He even advised not to take praise from such people. When someone is not satisfied with themselves, how can they praise you with utter honesty? You can still be friends with them, but don't count on their words. Marcus also reaffirmed that everything is in your power. How you take that opinion is what matters the most. You should not please everyone, as this is not your duty. However, Marcus even mentioned that you should also be aware of your own opinions. So, it's obvious that we should try our best to stop giving so much value to others' opinions. You simply don't need them. Look within instead.

Here are a couple more reasons why you should cast away others' opinions: when you're living your life based on others' opinions of you, you're giving up your own authentic inner voice, you're not being your true self, and you're not living up to your potential. You won't be happy living a life dictated by other people. The people who live by their inner voices are leaders. Those that don't are followers, and followers are never the first to do something of importance. You'll be more respected for being your own person and upholding your values, opinions, and morals.

Always say whatever is the truth. Someone who says the truth or who lives by their own terms can live peacefully on their own. You can respect yourself and be confident when you live in such a way, and other people will be respectful towards you. If you have a dream, fulfill it. No one else can stand in your shoes. Think about your purpose rather than what others think. Your own intellect or your inner voice can guide you to achieve what others have not. Such people may face objections and badmouthing. But every great man has faced his own set of challenges. They don't know what they're talking about all the time but they still do it, and they change the world.

Need some examples of outcasts and people who stood up for their beliefs even when everyone was against them? Just look at Galileo, Joan of Arc, Martin Luther, Robert Oppenheimer, Vincent Van Gogh, and Edgar Allan Poe.

Empower your true self. Remember that you can do anything. People will always judge you, and there isn't a single thing you can do about it, so do what you want anyway. Most people don't care what you're doing. They don't care because they're too wrapped up in their own drama. They're probably too worried thinking about what people think of them. Do you want proof? What's the first thing you look at when you look at a group photo? Probably yourself. People in social situations are the same exact way. They're focusing on themselves, not you.

Change Any Situation

How can you get a stoic mindset shift that you can implement straightaway? When you have a negative situation, it's very easy to flip that negative situation and make it positive. I'll start off with a quote from Epictetus: "Men are disturbed not by things, but by the view which they take of them." When something bad happens to you or a negative situation occurs, instead of dwelling on how negative it is, how bad it is, and how it makes you feel, think of it as an opportunity for you to practice one of the virtues.

So picture this: you've got a really bad cold or you're ill and you're just lying in bed. You can't go to work. Instead of contemplating and dwelling on how bad this makes you feel that there's nothing you can do, and that you're missing work, use it as an opportunity to do something productive for your life, like contemplate your existence, or meditating, or whatever it may be. All negative things that happen in life are just a chance for you to practice a virtue.

Control your life

Stoicism teaches us about being in control of our lives, not being victims, and taking extreme ownership of everything that happens to us. I believe that there's one other topic that goes hand-in-hand with that concept. But I believe that a lot of people are depressed because of these two things combined: first of all, they feel out of control and second of all, their perspective of life is out of whack. It's off and it's not correct because perspective is this amazing thing that completely changes how you view the world.

Happiness equals reality over expectations. This means that your happiness will increase as your reality gets better. I agree with this, and your actual reality will increase as your expectations get smaller. So if you can reduce your expectations of what's happening in your life, then you can become happier.

Now, the stoic ancient philosophers 2,000 years ago agreed with this. They had this idea of negative visualization that when you expect something negative to happen or at least expect something worse than what actually will happen, then that's better for you. Then, if that thing actually happens, you're prepared for it. And if something better than that thing that you're expecting to happen happens, then you're happier. Now, it's a minor thing that can be applied to your own life. Suppose you are about to move into a new flat or maybe new student accommodations. You are in your second year of college, and as you are moving into your room you do a little bit of negative visualization.

Imagine that your room will be horrible, tiny, and grim. When you move into this new room, you will be happy no matter what it will be like. Because obviously, student accommodation flats aren't that good. We all know that, but because you had negatively visualized what your room is going to be like, your expectations will be minimized so your happiness will end up increasing. This whole idea of perspective and shifting your perspective is such a powerful tool. You can also use it to become fulfilled when you face depression. And if you recognize how lucky you are, you are not depressed in a situation where someone else might be. It will increase your happiness. This should not be perceived as an offense to someone who is depressed. If you have depression, then you can look up to someone who can't walk or stand. This is what stoicism is in a nutshell. How can you be depressed when you recognize how lucky you are?

· · ·

Obviously, there are people with the chemical imbalances but for the people that don't have that genetic disposition, how can you be depressed when you've recognized how lucky you are? We live better than Kings lived years ago. We have many facilities that were lacking in the past. We are so lucky, and we're lucky because we're human. Think of all the different species you could have been. You could have been a camel. Even if you were the best camel in the world, even then you would not have as good as life as you have as a human. It's true! The best anything or the happiest something isn't as happy as you could be and isn't as lucky as you are. The fact that you're human and you're able to read this book is amazing. How lucky you are! Again, shift your perspective, recognize how lucky you are, and let gratitude flow through your body. If you want to be grateful, you've got to focus on the things that you're grateful for, because then you get to focus on only what you want to focus on, which should be being grateful. Take out five minutes a day and spend that time focusing on the things that you're grateful for. Don't just think logically about what you're grateful for, keep scanning your mind until you find something that triggers a feeling deep in your gut. Only then will you get to know what are you truly grateful for.

You Don't Feel Afraid of Death

Let us balance life's perks each day. You should count each day and analyze every second. Live each day as if it may be your last one. Everyone repeats it, but only a few people understand what it actually means. No, it does not mean that you should inject heroin because you're going to die anyway, and no it does not mean you should throw all morals out the window because the world is going to end. You should picture it just like this - you're a soldier leaving for deployment tomorrow. The day prior, you handle your business. You tie up any loose ends, you don't waste time arguing, you remind your loved ones that you love them and you're fully present. During the last few hours, you'll spend them with your family. The morning before you leave you're completely ready to go. You hope you will come back alive but you're fully aware there's a possibility that you will not. Live every single day starting with the day just like this. If you think of this method and utilize it every day in your meditation, then you will live a stoic life.

The connection between stoicism and death can be easily identified. Marcus said you can die anytime and anywhere. This knowledge can be a perfect exercise to calculate your words and actions. Every day as I start my meditation, I tell myself this quote, as it's the best quote for me. It grounds me into the present moment and the point of it. For me it speaks of urgency, appreciation, and humility.

It doesn't matter if you're rich or poor, blonde or brunette, whether you have lots of work to do or if you're on vacation. Whatever the case seems to be, a truck could still crash into you and you could still die. And this could happen anytime, such as tomorrow or even today. Take a few minutes to appreciate how short your life actually is in the grand scheme of things. Remember that the world still spins whether you were there or not. Too many people realize how precious life is when it's far too late. This is why Marcus Aurelius reminded himself more than five times in his personal diary about how short life actually is. By contemplating mortality, it will help you focus on what's important and it will help you realize how small your problems are and how much time you waste being someone you don't want to be.

BONUS MEDITATION

By doing this meditation, you will be able to respond quite effectively in any situation. You will become the leader of your own life. First, prepare yourself for this meditation. Start by making yourself comfortable as much as you can. Lay on a bed, a carpet, a reclining chair, or simply your seat on the train. Cover yourself with something to keep you warm and lay back in a comfortable position with your legs slightly apart and the palms of your hands facing upwards. You are going to practice deep relaxation for about half an hour and when you end this meditation, you will awaken feeling renewed and empowered.

Begin to take three deep breaths in order to begin the relaxation process. Inhale deeply filling your whole body with a sense of warmth and relaxation. Exhale as you release any tension in your face, your shoulders, and your whole physical body. Again, inhale deeply, filling your whole body with a sense of warmth and relaxation. Exhale as you release any tension and again inhale deeply, filling your body with warmth and relaxation. Exhale as you release any tension in your physical body.

Notice how relaxed you are feeling now, and as you are relaxing even deeper you will begin to notice your body feels as if it is sinking, as if it is so heavy that it is sinking into the chair or mattress. Next, you have to do a rotation of consciousness throughout your whole body. I will mention a few parts of your body and you will move your attention there, imagining a warm golden light in that area.

Let's begin with your head. Imagine a golden light all around your head. Now move this golden light to your forehead, your right eye, left eye, the right cheek, left cheek, and the lips. Now relax your jaw muscles. Relax your right shoulder and your left shoulder. Bring the golden light now to the abdomen area, the genital area, the whole right leg, the whole left leg and now bring your attention to your breathing.

As you inhale your abdomen rises. It inflates like a balloon, and as you exhale your abdomen falls. Notice this relaxing rise and fall. Now start counting your breaths backward from 12 to 0 as follows. I am inhaling 12, I am exhaling 12, I am inhaling 11, I am exhaling 11, and so on. Continue to count your breaths backward until zero.

When you reach the end, it's the time to bring to mind between five to ten things that made you grateful, joyful, and happy within the last 24 hours. If you can't think of enough incidents in the last 24 hours, expand to the last three days or the last week or last month. Think about these things that happen at work, things that happened when you were traveling, or in your free time. Pleasant and positive things that happen with your family or with your loved ones. It could be something big or it may be something small like a nice warm cup of hot tea. Express gratitude and bring back to mind the feeling of joy and the emotions you felt when these incidents occurred.

Take a few minutes to go through as many incidents of gratitude as you can think of, and as you imagine and bring back to mind these incidents and moments, make them as vivid as you can by incorporating all five senses. What will you hear, what will you taste, what or who will you touch, what will you smell, and picture the images. Make them as colorful and vivid as possible, and most importantly incorporate to the best of your ability the feeling of joy and happiness throughout your mind and body. Feel that feeling of gratitude from the top of your head to the bottom of your toes and know that when you express gratitude for beautiful moments in this life, you open the way for these moments to repeat themselves and to grow in terms of their magnitude.

Now we move on to release any negative charges. A negative charge is any feeling you might have towards a person or an incident towards which you might be harboring anger, resentment, jealousy, or any other toxicity. It could be a waiter who didn't treat you properly, a coworker who you had a disagreement with, a family member, or anyone else. It could be big or small, something that irritated you or something that is chronic and long-term. You will now mentally imagine that you are apologizing for any wrong that you brought to this person and see them apologizing back to you. On a deeper level we are all one, all connected, and any negative charge towards another living person or creature is in a way a charge against yourself. That's why we must rid ourselves of these negative charges or these toxic emotions.

When you finish expressing forgiveness to this person, see themselves forgiving you and you forgiving them. Imagine forgiveness moving from your heart outwards and then back towards your heart, and feel the calm and peace that engulfs your whole being. Of course, you need to note that when you're first starting out practicing this forgiveness exercise, you do it with situations where forgiveness is easier. Work your way upwards towards releasing more challenging feelings. Repeat this exercise with as many people with whom you have a negative charge. Simply repeat to yourself the phrases in your mind - "This thought is just an illusion, it really means nothing to me. I am free inside and nothing can harm me on the inside." Continue with "This thought is just an illusion. I can see the bigger picture of my life. I am free inside."

CONCLUSION

Stoicism is indeed the art of living. You will be surprised by the number of people who have been practicing Stoicism without knowing what it is. This book has taken you through a journey of discovery, and you are now prepared to make Stoicism a new way of life.

This book provided you with an introduction to stoicism and with several ways of integrating this philosophy in your life. You can practice stoicism in many situations and contexts in your life, from business or your profession to your romantic life. The bottom line is that stoicism implies an awareness of the fact that negative emotions are counterproductive. Its goal is teaching you how to maintain control over many aspects of your life by learning how to gain inner strength and independence from futile feelings and endeavors.

Practicing stoicism will help you gain more control over your life, stay perseverant and resistant under unfortunate or difficult circumstances, and keep unwanted emotions at bay.

Stoicism is also the perfect shield against people who could otherwise disturb you through their attitude or deeds.

Now that you have read this book, you will have a better understanding of the origins and concepts of the Stoic tradition. This knowledge will help you to develop the disciplines and virtues of Stoicism in your own life. The Stoic journey can be difficult and challenging at times, but the end result is absolutely worth it.

Whatever you choose, be happy with the result and be grateful that you even had the chance to live. Take ownership and responsibility for the life you have created and be content with it.